*Making Sense of Corru*

M000248039

Corruption is a serious threat to prosperity, democracy and human well-being, with mounting empirical evidence highlighting its detrimental effects on society. Yet defining this threat has resulted in profound disagreement, producing a multidimensional concept. Tackling this important and provocative topic, the authors provide an accessible and systematic analysis of how our understanding of corruption has evolved. They identify gaps in the research and make connections between related concepts such as clientelism, patronage, patrimonialism, particularism and state capture. A fundamental issue discussed is how the opposite of corruption should be defined. By arguing for the possibility of a universal understanding of corruption, and specifically what corruption is not, an innovative solution to this problem is presented. This book provides an accessible overview of corruption, allowing scholars and students alike to see the far-reaching place it has within academic research.

BO ROTHSTEIN is Professor of Government and Public Policy at the Blavatnik School of Government and Professorial Fellow of Nuffield College at University of Oxford. From 1995 to 2015, he held the August Röhss Chair in Political Science at the University of Gothenburg, where he was co-founder and head of The Quality of Government Institute. Since 2012 he has been a member of the Royal Swedish Academy of Sciences.

AIYSHA VARRAICH received a Master of Science degree from the International Administration and Global Governance Program at the University of Gothenburg in 2011. She worked as research assistant in the ANTICORRP project before entering the PhD program in political science at the University of Gothenburg in 2014. She is writing a thesis about clientelism and its effects on democratic processes within new democracies.

# Making Sense of Corruption

BO ROTHSTEIN
*University of Oxford, United Kingdom*

AIYSHA VARRAICH
*University of Gothenburg, Sweden*

CAMBRIDGE
UNIVERSITY PRESS

# CAMBRIDGE
## UNIVERSITY PRESS

University Printing House, Cambridge CB2 8BS, United Kingdom

One Liberty Plaza, 20th Floor, New York, NY 10006, USA

477 Williamstown Road, Port Melbourne, VIC 3207, Australia

314-321, 3rd Floor, Plot 3, Splendor Forum, Jasola District Centre, New Delhi-110025, India

79 Anson Road, #06-04/06, Singapore 079906

Cambridge University Press is part of the University of Cambridge.

It furthers the University's mission by disseminating knowledge in the pursuit of education, learning and research at the highest international levels of excellence.

www.cambridge.org
Information on this title: www.cambridge.org/9781316615270
DOI: 10.1017/9781316681596

© Bo Rothstein and Aiysha Varraich 2017

First published 2017

*A catalogue record for this publication is available from the British Library*

ISBN 978-1-107-16370-6 Hardback
ISBN 978-1-316-61527-0 Paperback

# Contents

# Figures and Tables

# Acknowledgements

This book is an outcome of a research program entitled 'Quality of Government (QoG) Institute' in the Department of Political Science at the University of Gothenburg. The QoG Institute was started in 2004 by Professors Sören Holmberg and Bo Rothstein to promote research about the nature, causes and consequences of quality in public institutions. We would like to thank all and every one of our many colleagues at the QoG Institute for great support, much encouragement and, not least, many high-quality critical comments to earlier drafts of various sections of this book. Bo Rothstein especially thanks Andreas Bågenholm, Carl Dahlström, Sören Holmberg, Anna Persson and Jan Teorell for their encouragement and support for this project. He also thanks Dalila Sabanic and Alice Johnsson for providing excellent administrative support and Francis Fukuyama for the possibility to present the ideas behind this book at two workshops organized by the Center for Democracy, Development and the Rule of Law at Stanford University. Aiysha Varraich thanks Dalila Sabanic, Richard Svensson and the entirety of the fifth floor group for constant encouragement on this project. She also thanks the QoG Institute for nurturing the intellectual curiosity of a fledgling scholar. Last but not least, she offers tremendous gratitude to her parents, who pushed her to question the big things in life.

The research for this book has been carried out to a large extent within a research program entitled 'Anti-Corruption Policies Revisited: Global Trends and European Responses to the Challenges of Corruption', generously funded by the European Union's Seventh Framework Program. We thank our many colleagues in this project for comments and support, especially Paul Heywood and Davide Torsello. We also hereby gratefully acknowledge the generous financial support from the Knut and Alice Wallenberg Foundation and the Swedish Research Council. Special thanks to Michael

Johnston for insightful remarks and encouragement on earlier versions of this manuscript.

A version of Chapter 9 was published previously in *Governance* (Rothstein 2015) and a version of Chapter 10 in *Third World Quarterly* (Rothstein 2014). We gratefully acknowledge the permission to include these versions in this book.

# 1 Corruption and the Relevance of Political Science

In an article entitled, 'Medical Care in Romania Comes at an Extra Cost', the *New York Times* (9 March 2009) reported the following story:

Alina Lungu, 30, said she did everything necessary to ensure a healthy pregnancy in Romania: she ate organic food, swam daily and bribed her gynaecologist with an extra $255 in cash, paid in monthly instalments handed over discreetly in white envelopes. She paid a nurse about $32 extra to guarantee an epidural and even gave about $13 to the orderly to make sure he did not drop the stretcher. But on the day of her delivery, she said, her gynaecologist never arrived. Twelve hours into labour, she was left alone in her room for an hour. A doctor finally appeared and found that the umbilical cord was wrapped twice around her baby's neck and had nearly suffocated him. He was born blind and deaf and is severely brain damaged ... Alina and her husband, Ionut, despair that the bribes they paid were not enough to prevent the negligence that they say harmed their son, Sebastian. 'Doctors are so used to getting bribes in Romania that you now have to pay more in order to even get their attention,' she said.[1]

Another example comes is a 2010 study from the World Bank entitled 'Silent and Lethal: How Quiet Corruption Undermines Africa's Development Efforts'. This study reports that nearly four out of five children in Tanzania who died of malaria had been taken by their parents to modern health facilities. The reason behind the very high mortality rate, of this often easily curable disease, is, according to the report, a 'range of manifestations of quiet corruption, including the absence of diagnostic equipment, drug pilfering, provider absenteeism, and very low levels of diagnostic effort'.

These are just two of what nowadays seem to be an infinite number of 'reports from the field' about the devastating consequences of corruption for the well-being of people around the world. The idea for this book is inspired by a statement made by the current President of the

---

[1] www.nytimes.com/2009/03/09/world/europe/09bribery.html?pagewanted=all.

World Bank, Jim Yong Kim, who in his speech of 19 December 2013 stated, 'In the developing world, corruption is public enemy no. 1.' As reported by Reuters,[2] this announcement showed how much this world-leading development organization had changed since the 1990s when the issue was taboo in the bank because it should not interfere in the internal politics of member states. By redefining corruption as also an economic problem, former World Bank President James Wolfensohn brought corruption into the limelight in the mid-1990s. Since then, many international aid and development organizations have become interested in issues related to the problem of corruption. Since corruption tends to be a sensitive issue, the 'coded language' for this policy re-orientation has been to stress the importance of 'good governance'. A typical statement comes from former United Nations General Secretary Kofi Annan: 'Good governance is perhaps the single most important factor in eradicating poverty and promoting development' (UN 1998). In academic circles, concepts such as 'institutional quality', 'quality of government' and 'state capacity' have also been used (Rothstein 2011; Smith 2007). However, as pointed out by Fukuyama (2013), a central problem in this discussion is a serious lack of conceptual precision. In the introduction to a recently published *Handbook of Political Corruption*, the editor writes that although corruption has attracted a lot of attention during the last twenty-five years, '[T]here remains a striking lack of scholarly agreement over even the most basic questions about corruption. Amongst the core issues that continue to generate disputes are the very definition of "corruption" as a concept' (Heywood 2015, p. 1; cf. Heywood 1977). The purpose of this book is to contribute to what seems to be an obvious need for conceptual clarification in this area. This, we want to underline, should not be seen as a purely intellectual or 'academic' enterprise. As stated by Sartori (1970, p. 1038), '[C]oncept formation stands prior to quantification.' Without conceptual precision, operationalization in order to find empirical measures for the level and degree of corruption in different societies becomes impossible. It follows that without being able to measure the problem, we cannot compare the level of corruption between societies or study changes over time. If so, we will not be able to find out what may work as remedies for corruption (cf. Møller and Skaaning 2014).

2  www.reuters.com/article/us-worldbank-corruption-idUSBRE9BI11P20131219.

However, we would like to underline that apart from the specific research and policy interests in such a conceptual project, there is another important rationale for why a discussion about how to theorize, define and measure corruption and what may constitute the opposite of corruption is important. This argument is basically empirical and has to do with unexpected and, for many, including the authors of this book, also normatively unwelcome results.

The problem pertains to the effects of democratization. The waves of democracy that have swept across the globe since the mid-1970s have brought representative democracy to places where it seemed inconceivable fifty, thirty, or even ten years ago. More countries than ever are now, by the most sophisticated measures used, classified as being democratic, and more people than ever live in what counts as democracies (Teorell 2010). This is certainly something to celebrate, but there are also reasons to be disappointed. One such example is South Africa, which miraculously managed to end apartheid in 1994 without falling into a full-scale civil war. As Nelson Mandela said in one of his speeches, the introduction of democracy would not only liberate people but also greatly improve their social and economic situation. The slogan that his political party, the African National Congress (ANC), used in the first democratic elections was 'a better life for all' (Mandela 1994, p. 414; cf. Greenberg 2009). However, available statistics give a surprisingly bleak picture for this promise. Since 1994, the country has not managed to improve the time that children on average go to school by a single month. Economic inequality remains at record levels, life expectancy is down by almost six years and the number of women who die in childbirth has more than doubled.[3] Simply put, for many central measures of human well-being, the South African democracy has not delivered (Rothstein and Tannenberg 2015). Another example is provided by Amartya Sen in an article comparing 'quality of life' in China and India. His disappointing conclusion is that by most standard measures of human well-being, communist-autocratic Peoples' Republic of China now clearly outperforms liberal and democratically governed India (Sen 2011). Using a set of thirty standard measures of national levels of human well-being from between 75 and 169 countries, Holmberg and Rothstein (2011) find only weak, or no, or sometimes even negative, correlations between these standard measures of

---

[3] Data from the Quality of Government Data Bank (Teorell et al. 2013).

human well-being and the level of democracy as just defined. Maybe the most compelling evidence about the lack of positive effects of democracy on human well-being comes from a study about child deprivation by Halleröd et al. (2013) using data measuring seven aspects of child poverty (i.e. access to safe water, food, sanitation, shelter, education, healthcare and information) from sixty-eight low- and middle-income countries for no less than 2,120,734 cases (children). The result of this large study shows that there is no positive effect of democracy on the level of child deprivation for any of the seven indicators.

This bleak picture of the effect of democratization on measures of prosperity, population health and other central aspects of human well-being is confirmed by many other studies (for reference to this literature, see Rothstein and Tanneberg 2015). The picture that emerges from the available measures is this: representative democracy is not a safe cure against severe poverty, child deprivation, economic inequality, illiteracy, being unhappy or unsatisfied with one's life, infant mortality, short life expectancy, maternal mortality, access to safe water or sanitation, gender inequality, low school attendance for girls, low interpersonal trust or low trust in parliament (Rothstein and Tannenberg 2015). Why is this so? Larry Diamond gave one explanation in a paper presented at the National Endowment for Democracy in the United States as it celebrated its first twenty-five years of operations:

There is a spectre haunting democracy in the world today. It is bad governance – governance that serves only the interests of a narrow ruling elite. Governance that is drenched in corruption, patronage, favouritism, and abuse of power. Governance that is not responding to the massive and long-deferred social agenda of reducing inequality and unemployment and fighting against dehumanizing poverty. Governance that is not delivering broad improvement in people's lives because it is stealing, squandering, or skewing the available resources. (Diamond 2007, p. 19)

If we follow Diamond's shift of focus from representative democracy and turn to various measures of corruption, quality of government and 'good governance', the picture of what politics can do for human well-being changes dramatically. For example, the aforementioned study on child deprivation finds strong effects from measures of quality of government on four of seven indicators on child deprivation (i.e. lack of safe water, malnutrition, lack of access to healthcare and lack of

What about corr. of democr & qual of force

access to information), controlling for gross domestic product (GDP) per capita and a number of basic individual-level variables (Halleröd et al. 2013). Other studies largely confirm that various measures of control of corruption and quality of government have strong effects on almost all standard measures of human well-being, including subjective measures of life satisfaction (aka 'happiness') and social trust (Holmberg and Rothstein 2011, 2012, 2015; Norris 2012; Ott 2010; Rothstein and Stolle 2008). Recent studies also find that absence of violence, in the form of interstate and civil wars, is strongly affected by measures of quality of government and more so than by the level of democracy (Lapuente and Rothstein 2014; cf. Teorell 2015). In addition, as Sarah Chayes (2015) points out, corruption is an important cause behind the rise of terrorist and insurgent military groups that has hitherto been ignored both by research and in the academic analyses of security policy.

Some may argue that the normative reasons for representative democracy should not be performance measures such as the ones mentioned earlier but political legitimacy. If people have the right to change their government through 'free and fair elections', they will find their system of rule legitimate (Rothstein 2009). Here comes maybe an even bigger surprise from empirical research, namely, that democratic rights do not seem to be the most important cause behind people's perception of political legitimacy (Gilley 2006, 2009). Based on comparative survey data, several recent studies show that 'performance' or 'output' measures such as control of corruption, government effectiveness and the rule of law trump democratic rights in explaining political legitimacy (Dahlberg and Holmberg 2014; Gilley 2009; Gjefsen 2012). As stated by Bruce Gilley, '[T]his clashes with standard liberal treatments of legitimacy that give overall priority to democratic rights' (2006, p. 58). Our argument is certainly not that representative democracy is unimportant but that without a reasonably competent, impartial, uncorrupted, honest and effective public administration, representative democracy is unlikely to deliver or increase human well-being.

Our normative starting point follows the principles of justice launched by the economist and philosopher Amartya Sen. His capability approach to justice is based on two basic ideas. The first is that the freedom to achieve well-being is of central moral importance, and the second is that this requires that individuals have resources that can be converted into capabilities so that they have real opportunities to do and be what they themselves have reason to value (Sen 2009). This has been translated into various metrics of what should count as 'human well-being'. This is not the place for a lengthy discussion or comparison of these metrics. Instead, we choose to assume that most of us would prefer to live in a country where few newborn babies die, where most children survive their fifth birthday, where almost all ten-year-olds can read, where people live a long and reasonably healthy life, where child deprivation is low, where few women die when giving birth, where the percentage of people living in severe poverty is low and where many report being reasonably satisfied with their lives. We may also like to live in a society in which people think that the general ethical standard among their fellow citizens is reasonably high, implying that they perceive corruption to be fairly uncommon and that they think that 'most people in general' can be trusted (Holmberg and Rothstein 2015). If this is the case, then the question of whether political science can be relevant becomes a question of the extent to which the discipline can contribute to increased human well-being or, to paraphrase the title of another book in this approach, whether the discipline can contribute to our understanding of why some societies are more 'successful' than others (Hall and Lamont 2009). Our purpose is thus to deliberately cross the line between the normative (value) and empirical (fact) approaches in the social science. As argued by Gerring and Ysenowitz (2006, p. 105):

[W]e cannot conceptualize the scholarly significance of a theoretical framework or a particular empirical puzzle without also contemplating its relevance to society, its normative importance. This underlying feature of social science provides the missing organizing element, without which the activity of social science is, quite literally, meaningless.

Thus, if the relevance of research in the social sciences in general (and particularly for political science) is understood as how it may improve human well-being and/or improve political legitimacy, research has to a large extent been focusing on the least important part of the political system, namely, how 'access to power' is organized (i.e. electoral and representative democracy and processes of democratization). This focus on 'input' variables (e.g. elections, democratization processes, party systems) ignores what we consider to be the more important part of the state machinery for increasing human well-being, namely, how power is exercised or, in other words, the quality of how the state manages to govern society (Rothstein 2011). As argued by Fukuyama

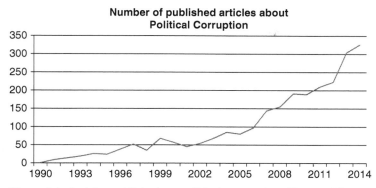

**Number of published articles about
Political Corruption**

**Figure 1.1** Articles published on political corruption. (Source: Thomson Web of Science 2015.)

(2013), this seems to have been driven by an underlying ideological view inspired by neoclassical economics, particularly strong in the United States, that emphasizes the need to limit, check and control (and often also minimize) the state, which is basically seen as a 'predatory' organization. In other words, how to 'tame the beast' has been the central focus, not what 'the animal' can achieve. The result is that the quality of the administrative part of the state, which we now know is of the outmost importance for increasing human well-being, has been severely under-studied, under-theorized and under-measured both in economics and in political science. One effect of this was that until the late 1990s, the interest in researching political corruption in political science and related disciplines such as economics, public administration and policy analysis was very modest. As shown in Figure 1.1, the total number of articles published in journals listed in one of the major bibliographical databases (Thomson ISI) containing the term 'political corruption' in the title, as keyword or in the abstract for the year 1992 was fourteen. Since the database covers about 1,700 scholarly social science journals, each publishing about fifty articles per year, this is a surprisingly low number.

As stated as late as 2006 by one of the most prominent political scientists in this field, Michael Johnston: 'American political science as an institutionalized discipline has remained steadfastly uninterested in corruption for generations' (2006, p. 809). This seems to be a correct observation shown by the fact that the discipline's flagship journal – the

*American Political Science Review* – in total contains only two articles about political corruption for the years 1992–2006 (out of a total of 666 published articles in the previously mentioned database). This lack of an interest in issues about corruption can also be observed from the many handbooks in political science that have been published during the last decade. None of the following ten *Oxford Handbooks* published between 2006 and 2014 have a chapter, a section of a chapter or even an index entry for the term 'corruption':

1. *The Oxford Handbook of Political Science*
2. *The Oxford Handbook of Comparative Politics*
3. *The Oxford Handbook of Public Policy*
4. *The Oxford Handbook of Comparative Institutional Analysis*
5. *The Oxford Handbook of Political Theory*
6. *The Oxford Handbook of the Welfare State*
7. *The Oxford Handbook of Political Institutions*
8. *The Oxford Handbook of Law and Politics*
9. *The Oxford Handbook of Political Psychology*
10. *The Oxford Handbook of Political Leadership*

This lack of interest in research about corruption in political science stands in sharp contrast to what seems to be the opinion of the 'general public'. According to a British Broadcasting Company (BBC) poll in 2010 surveying 13,353 respondents in twenty-six countries, corruption is the most talked about issue globally, surpassing issues such as climate change, poverty and unemployment (Katzarova 2011). Or type the search word 'corruption' on the BBC News website, and a staggering 8,972 hits are reached. The same search on the well-known journal *The Economist's* website gets you over 48,000 hits for 'corruption'. The overwhelming presence of the topic of corruption is not limited to the realm of the Internet – suffice to mention that the 'Arab Spring' started with an incident about corruption (Chayes 2015). Additionally, the huge demonstrations and protests in Brazil in 2013 were to a large extent concerned with issues of 'clean' government.[4] Thus, from a very modest position lasting until the second half of the 1990s, political corruption has now become a very central topic for many leading international organizations and has grown considerably in academia. Corruption has been recognized as a valid and challenging subject,

---

[4] 'Taking to the street', *The Economist*, 22 June 2013.

putting it high on the priority agenda of both political/social scientists and policymakers (Chayes 2015; Heywood 2014; Jain 2001). This is evidenced by corruption's treatment hand in hand with the 'good governance' agenda promoted by various international bodies such as the World Bank, International Monetary Fund (IMF) and so on. Further evidence is in the form of the establishment of anti-corruption units (as well as campaigns) within many international organizations such as the United Nations, the European Union and the African Union. Important non-government organizations (NGOs) such as Transparency International and the Natural Resource Governance Institute work hard to bring attention to the detrimental effects of corruption. Several new legal instruments have also been established by national governments as well as at the international level[5]. During the last fifteen years, it is fair to say that the number of international and national policy organizations that are engaged in various types of anti-corruption programmes have reached the point where it is possible to speak about an international anti-corruption regime (McCoy and Heckel 2001; Mungiu-Pippidi 2011, 2015; Wedel 2014). However, this presence has taken its time to reach the state it is at today.

In contrast to the current hype surrounding corruption, the *concept* itself has until recently received surprisingly little attention (Miller 2011). Most papers begin with a brief, typically one-sentence definition and then move on to discussing its aspects. A thorough exploration and discussion at the conceptual level remains scant. However, lately, the discussion of what should be considered the opposite off corruption, such as 'good governance', 'state capacity' and 'quality of government', has become intense (Agnafors 2013; Andrews 2013; Fukuyama 2013; Heywood and Rose 2015; Philp 2015; Rothstein and Teorell 2008). Recognizing this lacuna in the scholarship pertaining to the conceptualization of corruption, our intention is to map the landscape of different conceptualizations of corruption and related concepts such as clientelism, patronage, particularism, state capture and patrimonialism. In

---

[5]　The United Nations Convention against Corruption (UNCAC), 2003; European Council Convention against Corruption (both criminal and civil), 1997; Inter-American Convention against Corruption, 1996; African Union Convention on Preventing and Combating Corruption, 2003; OECD Convention on Combating Bribery of Foreign Public Officials in International Business Transactions, 1997; Southern African Development Community Protocol Against Corruption, 2001.

this, a central ambition is to specify how this family of concepts is connected. Secondly, we want to specify what is to be considered as the opposite of corruption. If corruption is a special form of decay of the political system, we need to know what the opposite of this process is. Thirdly, we aim to fill the gaps that can be identified in the absence of a single unified definition of corruption. This is a daunting task because a large number of policy organizations and academics – we dare say the absolute majority – work with a relativistic and multidimensional definition (see e.g. Agnafors 2013). A fourth task is that we will also analyze the under-developed link that we have found between the anti-corruption discourse and the human rights agenda and suggest avenues of exploration/direction for the future of the conceptual development of corruption. Lastly, the Peoples' Republic of China has been a notorious troublemaker in this field of research. The reason is that while the country has had exceptional economic growth and massive improvements in the standard measures of human well-being, during the last three decades, it is also known for having fairly high levels of corruption. Our analysis will show that while corruption is a problem in China, the way the country's public administration works for producing valued outcomes has to a large extent been misunderstood.

## Corruption as Taboo

The emergence of corruption as a subject matter within academia has been a long journey. Until about the mid-1990s, corruption as a topic was more or less taboo – both in research and in policy circles, substantiated by the fact that the use of the word itself was referred to as the 'c-word' (Shah 2007, p. 249). In the late 1960s, Swedish economist (and Nobel Laureate) Gunnar Myrdal pointed out that the term 'corruption' was 'almost taboo as a research topic and was rarely mentioned in scholarly discussions of the problems of government and planning' (Myrdal 1968, p. 937). In his research about social and economic development in India, Myrdal pointed at the problem of the 'soft state', a concept that included both corruption and ineffectiveness. Although Myrdal's focus in the quoted article was on South Asia, this reasoning can be extrapolated to understand the hesitance, until at least the late 1990s, of doing research on corruption. There are different reasons forwarded for the lack of an academic focus on corruption, especially for research concerning developing countries – one being a general bias of 'diplomacy in research'. This 'diplomacy' stems from the historical setting when Myrdal's article was published, that is, in the midst of the 'Third Wave of Democratisation' that took place from about 1974 to the late 1990s (Huntington 1991). This was a sensitive time, during which both academic and policy circles engaged in the avoidance of corruption as a topic for fear of being labelled 'imperialist', 'Western', 'post-colonialist' or simply self-righteous. Another reason for the absence of corruption research was what can be labelled as 'geographic morality'. According to this line of thinking, the prevalent attitude was one of 'us' and 'them', effectively the Western world (liberal democracies) versus the (then) Third World (non-democracies and countries in transition, such as the former colonial states). This attitude resulted in externalizing the issue of corruption as a problem that does not exist in the Western world but is limited to the Third World. This is neatly summarized by Kotkin and Sajó:

Corruption seemed prevalent, even inevitable, not everywhere but in certain societies; especially in the West's colonies and other less developed parts of the world ... The temptation to identify corruption with alien societies, with the other, has always been irresistible. (2002, p. 25)

The fact that Myrdal's essay formed part of a lengthy book entitled, *An Enquiry into the Poverty of Nations*, which focused on the Asian continent, is evidence of the prevalent prejudice of the time, which may explain the need felt by many academics to remain 'neutral' or 'diplomatic', thereby avoiding stirring up a sensitive issue like corruption. Matters were of a similar nature on the policy front, where this type of reasoning was also used by international organizations such as the World Bank, effectively avoiding research and discussion of the topic. The official stance of these organizations was that problems related to corruption constituted 'a national issue' that was beyond the purview of the organization's mandate that stated that interference into national political issues was not allowed. As Pearson points out, the reluctance of these institutions to address corruption can also be attributed to their 'perception of themselves as politically neutral, the limitations of their charters and because of the sensitivities of many of their member States' (Pearson 2013, p. 31). The Cold War alliances are also very likely to have played a role in this denial of the problem. None of the main parties in this conflict wanted to accuse their partners in developing countries of being engaged in or tolerating corruption.

As mentioned earlier, all this changed when former World Bank President James D. Wolfensohn redefined corruption as an economic problem in the mid-1990s. In an interview in 2005, he stated: 'Ten years ago, when I came here, the Bank never talked about corruption, and now we are doing programs in more than a hundred countries, and it is a regular subject for discussion' (World Bank 2010). It is noteworthy that it was a policy organization that broke the 'taboo' surrounding corruption and that academia, and not least the political science discipline, for the most part came around later.

## Breaking the Taboo

An early effort to break the taboo against corruption was the publication in 1970 of Arnold Heidenheimer's *Political Corruption: Readings in Comparative Analysis*. In this work, Heidenheimer analyzed the concept through three separate categories, focusing on the public realm: public office, public interest and public opinion. He defined the three as follows:

1. *Public-office-centred definitions:* '[D]efinitions of corruption that relate most essentially to the concept of public office and to deviations from norms binding upon its incumbents ... Corruption, while being tied particularly to the act of bribery, is a general term covering misuse of authority as a result of considerations of personal gain, which need not be monetary.'
2. *Market-centred definitions:* '[A] corrupt civil servant regards his public office as a business, the income of which he will ... seek to maximise. The office then becomes a – maximising unit' (Van Klaveren 1957), or as Leff (1964) points out: 'Corruption is an extra-legal institution used by individuals or groups to gain influence over the actions of the bureaucracy. As such the existence of corruption per se indicates only that these groups participate in the decision-making process to a greater extent than would otherwise be the case.'
3. *Public-interest-centred definitions:* 'The pattern of corruption can be said to exist whenever a power holder who is charged with doing certain things, i.e. who is a responsible functionary or officeholder, is by monetary or other rewards not legally provided for, induced to take actions which favour whoever provides the rewards and thereby does damage to the public and its interests.'

The first step towards breaking the taboo, apart from the publication of the work itself, was the re-labelling of 'corruption' to 'political corruption', bringing the term within the ambit of the political realm. This effectively lifted the concept to a normative and philosophical level, reinforcing the term as, above all, a politically polysemic term, broadening the meaning of the word to be 'linked with system decay' (Heidenheimer et al. 1989, p. 12). The subject now fell within the realm not only of the social sciences but also more specifically within the political science field, providing impetus to scholars to engage in corruption research. The political nature was now applicable to all political entities (states), reinforcing the political range of the term (Génaux 2004). In other words, corruption as a subject for research was applicable to all nations, whether developing or industrialized. What also helped to break the taboo was Heidenheimer's application of this newly established framework in his analysis of the United States during the Watergate scandal period. This effectively shook the concept loose from the political bias that until then had surrounded corruption and led to an opening of the floodgates of conceptualizations.

Before elaborating on the many extant conceptualizations of corruption, it is imperative to note that the majority of corruption studies and policies focus on the public sphere, not the private. The reasons for this  are manifold. First of all, the public sphere is that within which the citizenry has a direct linkage to the state through payment of taxes and the provision (or, due to corruption, non-provision) of public goods. In lieu of this, when public-sector corruption takes place, the chief argument in favour of the public-sector focus as fundamental is that corruption weakens the accountability mechanism available to a state's citizens, thereby effectively weakening the collective action tool available to the population. Furthermore, Andvig et al. (2001) argue that public-sector corruption remains the centre of attention mainly because it acts as a prerequisite for controlling private-sector corruption. Arguments from another angle pertain to the subversion of the public good as the central feature for focus on the public-sector corruption versus private, wherein corruption occurs when those who are in charge of societies' 'public goods' transform those goods into their private goods (Booth and Cammack 2013; Rothstein and Torsello 2014). Although the aforementioned arguments focus on corruption in the public sphere, it is of interest to note, as Johnston (2013) points out, that the level at which corruption is investigated is the private domain as it occurs at the individual level (i.e. the private level), whereas the classical republican understanding focuses on corruption as a collective action problem (Persson et al. 2013; cf. Marguette 2014). An imperative point is that all the aforementioned arguments focus on corruption at the 'output side' of the political system (mainly the public administration, the public services and the judicial system) and not the 'input side' (parties, parliaments), which was the initial problem where exercise of power was not analyzed.

Corruption usually occurs at the intersection of public and private spheres, for example, where individuals engaging in corrupt behaviour within private companies, for their own interest, affect the taxpayers' money. One such example is the latest financial crisis of 2008, where the actions of the private banking sector affected taxpayer money when the banks needed to be bailed out by the respective states. An example given by the then lead economist at the World Bank, Daniel Kaufmann, is a meeting held in April 2004 where the CEOs of the (then) five big investment banks on Wall Street persuaded the US Securities and Exchange Commission to relax the Glass-Steagall Act, the regulation that stipulated the level of their financial reserves. This policy had been established to prevent the type of crisis that occurred four years later. Kaufmann coined the term 'legal corruption' for describing what happened and concluded his analysis with the following words: 'If anybody thought that the governance and corruption challenge was a monopoly of the developing world ... that notion has been disposed completely' (Kaufmann 2008, 2011). This has been concisely summarized in a comment by the World Bank:

> [T]he problem of corruption lies at the intersection of the public and private sectors. It is a two-way street. Private interests, domestic and external, wield their influence through illegal means to take advantage of opportunities for corruption and rent seeking, and public institutions succumb to these and other sources of corruption in the absence of credible restraints. (World Bank 1997, p. 102)

This intersection of public and private sectors is a 'grey zone' that is underexplored in the literature as well as in policy circles. A stark example of this grey zone where public and private lines are blurred is the concept of 'state capture'. State capture focuses on how the private sector exerts influence over the public sphere, mainly by shaping the

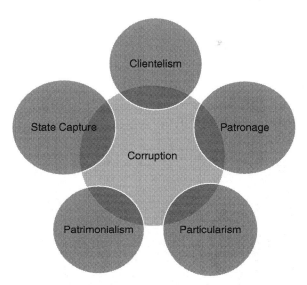

**Figure 1.2** Corruption as an umbrella concept.

formation of the basic rules of the game (i.e. laws, rules, decrees and regulations), whether this be through illicit and non-transparent private payments to public officials/politicians or politicians exercising power (see Chapter 8). The corruption in this case takes place on the input side of the political system, unlike other types of corruption that occur at the output side. Some scholars have labelled this type of corruption 'institutional', by which they imply that the rules of the democratic system are systematically biased so as not to favour any general or public interest but instead various private interests (Lessig 2013; Thompson 1995). As will be argued in Chapter 10, it turns out to be difficult to find a clear and precise demarcation line for the 'input side' between what is to be considered illegitimate influence through money or other forms of power and what is to be seen as legitimate political mobilization. For example, if a pharmaceutical company makes a direct payment to a Member of Parliament in exchange for her or his vote, this would be seen by almost all observers as political corruption. However, if a union movement supports a political party by giving money to the party and in exchange expects and gets legislation that makes it easier for the unions to recruit and keep members, the case is not that clear. Many would say that this is not corruption but 'just politics'.

Today, corruption has been explored within a majority of social science disciplines. However, there is a gap within the current research where the use of corruption as an umbrella concept is for the most part absent (Varraich 2014). Our intention is to fill this gap by developing a 'core understanding' that acts as a connecter to ancillary concepts with which it is regularly connected, such as clientelism, patronage, state capture and patrimonialism. Our idea is to use corruption as an umbrella concept for this family of related concepts, as illustrated in Figure 1.2 (cf. Varraich 2014). The starting point will be to investigate the different conceptualizations of corruption that exist within the different academic disciplines. This serves as a primer for understanding the overlaps that exist between the academic disciplines themselves before moving on to the exploration and analysis of the similarity shared by corruption and its 'sister' concepts.

# 2 | *Mapping-Related Disciplines*

Corruption has been conceptualized and defined in different academic disciplines at different times, with the result that each discipline has developed its own understanding pertaining to the nuanced outlook each discipline provides, without reaching consensus over a definition or conceptualization. This chapter serves the purpose of briefly introducing how corruption became a matter of interest in each respective discipline, along with its conceptualization/definition, but also how it has been handled empirically by each of them.

## Corruption as an Economic Issue

As shown in Chapter 1, well into the 1990s, the problem with corruption was reflected neither within the policy circles nor in the policies for development that were being fleshed out. This was especially evident within major international policy institutions such as the World Bank. The conceptualization of corruption from the economic perspective gained momentum once corruption was identified as a deterrent to economic growth, particularly in developing and transition nations (Jain 2001). Studying corruption as an economic phenomenon relates not only to the 'economic advantage' in the form of bribes and kickbacks but also to subfields such as public finance, industrial organization and the economics of crime and the role of the 'invisible foot' in these subfields (Lambsdorff 2007; Rose-Ackerman and Søreide 2011). As Andvig et al. (2001, p. 6) make clear, by looking at the kinds of resources transferred, a distinction has been made between corruption in economic terms and corruption in social terms. Economic corruption takes place in a market-like situation and entails an exchange of cash or material goods, effectively making market-centred definitions a morally neutral or 'rational' (Hodgkinson 1997, p. 22) way of applying economic methods and models for the analysis of politics (Philp 1997, p. 48). As Underkuffler (2005, p. 21) clarifies, '[C]orrupt acts, qua corrupt acts, are neither good nor bad; they are simply the manifestation of interests, which are equal – in any normative sense – to any other interests in the competitive sea.' However, in the mid-1990s within academia, the concept was re-formulated as an economic problem. One such market-centred formulation is that offered by Van Klaveren:

A corrupt civil servant regards his public office as a business the income of which he will ... seek to maximise. The office then becomes a 'maximising unit.' The size of his income depends ... upon the market situation and his talents for finding the point of maximal gain on the public's demand curve. (Cited in Johnston 1996, p. 323)

Social corruption, however, is conventionally understood as an integrated element of clientelism, where social aspects are involved, that is, the way people relate to each other, one form of which is interpersonal domination. As Médard (1998, p. 308) elaborates, '[C]orruption takes many forms, clientelism, nepotism, ethnic and other favouritism are all variants of corruption, in social terms.' Another example of social corruption is as a social condition, pointing to its effect upon the law. Ritner succinctly demonstrates this in his analysis of corruption in the writings of Niccolò Machiavelli:

Corruption is the loss of military virtue and therefore the inability to maintain the social cohesion and enforce the laws of the state. The laws of the state become corrupt when sects of persons in positions of authority misuse their magistracies for the purpose of personal or sectional gain, or in a way that circularly harms the maintenance and development of the virtue of the people. (Cited in Ritner 2011, p. 18)

On the policy side, the re-formulation of corruption as an economic issue brought it within the purview of the mandates governing the institutions of the World Bank and the International Monetary Fund (IMF), as well as other international organizations. The market-centred definition of corruption neatly severed itself from the behavioural definitions that surround the public office and public interest definitions. As a result, the concept of corruption was seen as no longer constituting a national political problem but as an *economic* problem that crossed borders and affected us all (Rose-Ackerman 1999). The 'Bretton Woods twins' soon treated corruption as an obvious aspect of the 'good governance' agenda that was promoted as part and parcel of the policy, once again aimed at the developing world.[1]

Corruption research within economics and especially anti-corruption policy have leaned back on this research and have to a large extent been guided by an economic approach called the 'principal-agent theory'. Corruption, the theory says, is a situation which can be fixed if the honest 'principal' changes the incentives for his or her dishonest corrupt 'agents' so that they will find it more to their interest to stay away from corruption (Klitgaard 1988; Rose-Ackerman 1999). To put it simply, since the 'agents' are thought to be rational utility maximizers, when the incentive system is changed so that the fear of being caught gets higher than the greed that drives corrupt behaviour, things would go well. Trying to answer why, for the most part, anti-corruption policies have failed, Persson et al. (2013) point at the shortcomings in this theory. The main problem, they argue, is that the principal-agent theory relies on a certain type of actor (the benevolent and ethical 'principal') who is *not* a rational self-interested utility maximizer. This implies that the main 'mover' that the theory points at is the type of agent who is not supposed to exist according to the theory itself (cf. Besley 2007). This makes the theory problematic because in most systemically corrupt systems, one should take for granted that it is the actors at 'the top' who are the presumed principals who earn most of the 'rents' from corruption. Obviously, such principals will have little incentives to change the incentives for their opportunistic agents who are engaged in corruption. Another obvious problem with the principal-agent theory is that if erasing corruption were just a matter of changing incentives, the problem should have been fixed long ago, since there is no lack of knowledge of how to structure an incentive system.

As an alternative, Persson et al. (2013) suggest that systemic corruption should be understood in line with the theory of 'collective action', much like Elinor Ostrom's research on common-pool resources (Ostrom 1990). In such a situation, agents are not motivated by utility maximization but by what they perceive will be the most likely strategy

---

[1] This can be seen from the policies surrounding the 'good governance' agenda and the various conditional loans dependent upon fulfilment of good governance criteria as well as the different bodies within the United Nations that got formed and centred in the target countries – such as the democratic governance sections created within the United Nations Development Programme, which strictly focus on the developing nations of the world (see Bracking 2007).

of most other agents in their society. This idea of understanding human behaviour as based on reciprocity instead of rational utility maximization has gained substantial support in recent experimental research showing that agents are willing to do 'the right thing' provided that they have reason to expect others to do the same (Bicchieri and Xiao 2009; cf. March and Olsen 1989). As stated by Fehr and Fischbacher (2005, p. 81): 'If people believe that cheating on taxes, corruption and abuses of the welfare state are widespread, they themselves are more likely to cheat on taxes, take bribes or abuse welfare state institutions.' From this collective action–based approach to corruption follows policy solutions that are very different from those of the principal-agent theory, which focus on creating incentives. Effective policies against corruption need to send a 'big bang' type of signal to society that may make most agents who are engaged in corruption believe that most other agents are willing to change (Rothstein 2011; Uslaner and Rothstein 2016). It should be noted that philosopher John Rawls, to whom we will come back in Chapter 10, does address this collective-action problem in his famous book, *A Theory of Justice*. Writing about the possibility to create a political system that will be supported by its members because they perceive the system to be justly arranged, Rawls recognized a danger to such a 'justice as fairness' system even when the members perceive of the arrangements as just:

For although men know that they share a common sense of justice and that each wants to adhere to existing arrangements, they may nevertheless lack full confidence in one another. They may suspect that some are not doing their part, and so they may be tempted not to do theirs. The general awareness of these temptations may eventually cause the scheme to break down. The suspicion that others are not honoring their duties and obligations is increased by the fact that, in absence of the authoritative interpretation and enforcement of the rules, it is particularly easy to find excuses for breaking them. (Rawls 1971, p. 240)

The implication is in perfect accordance with the results that have come out from the experimental work cited earlier. In our case, even if 'all' agents would prefer a system free of corruption, they may still be tempted to take part in corrupt activities if they perceive that this is what most other agents in their situation will do.

The most important contribution from economics to the understanding of corruption is the focus on institutions or 'the rules of the game'.

The lead person in this approach has been economic historian Douglass C. North. By pointing at the importance of institutions, North challenged the dominating view that structural factors such as economic power structures, natural resources endowment and geographical location were key in explaining variations in social and economic outcomes (North 1990).

Broadly understood, institutions refer to formal and informal rules that influence all actors and sectors in a society – be they citizens, organizations, the economy and so on. At the centre of such rules are governments, which not only create, administer and enforce the rules but whose very operations are also legitimized by some and constrained by others (Andrews 2013). These 'rules of the game' affect the size, procedures and reach of governments, e.g., formal budget rules, property rights, taxation systems, regulation on access to information and also the corresponding informal rules, such as social trust, political legitimacy and norms about information disclosure. These institutions are all connected to governments in one way or the other. Institutional theory holds that different institutional configurations generate different incentive structures, which, in turn, lead to different behaviours, resulting in different outcomes. Since the launch of institutionalism, the theoretical debate in development economics has by and large shifted in favour of the importance of institutions, to a point where there is close to a consensus that the quality of institutions matters more than anything else in terms of impact on development (Acemoglu and Robinson 2008; World Bank 2002), or in the words of Rodrik et al. (2004), '[I]nstitutions rule.' The difference between this new 'institutional economics' and the established neoclassical paradigm has been neatly captured by Dani Rodrik in the following way:

The encounter between neo-classical economics and developing societies served to reveal the institutional underpinnings of market economies. A clearly delineated system of property rights, a regulatory apparatus curbing the worst forms of fraud, anti-competitive behavior, and moral hazard, a moderately cohesive society exhibiting trust and social cooperation, social and political institutions that mitigate risk and manage social conflicts, the rule of law and clean government – these are social arrangements that economists usually take for granted, but which are conspicuous by their absence in poor countries ... Hence it became clear that incentives would not work or generate perverse results in the absence of adequate institutions. (Rodrik 1999, p. 16; cf. Rodrik 2007, p. 97)

Although corruption is not always a central theme in this approach, it is clear that control of corruption serves as an underlying theme for the long list of institutions that Rodrik argues are necessary for creating well-functioning markets. Moreover, it points to a discussion of how to define the opposite of corruption, which has to be some form of institutions of a certain quality (Olson 1996). The issue then becomes how to define what this quality is about. To connect back to the quote from Rawls earlier, they should be institutions that instil confidence in most people that most other people will 'do their part' and that they thereby refrain from falling for the 'temptation' to do otherwise.

## Corruption in Legal Studies

A parallel development to the one described for economics and institutions earlier can be detected in the field of legal studies in the 1990s. Here we can see an upsurge of conceptualizations of corruption within the legal field, where Joseph La Palombara's definition of corruption stated that it was to be defined as 'any act performed by officials when departing from their legal obligations in exchange for personal advantages' (La Palombara 1994, p. 330). This definition helps to limit the concept of corruption to stay within the framework of the law, providing guidelines as to which criteria cover and which do not cover corrupt acts – explaining why the legal conception of corruption is used in many empirical studies. However, this approach/conception has been criticized as too broad and also as too narrow. As Underkuffler (2005, p. 21) points out, '[T]he idea of "corruption-as-illegality" . . . suffer[s] from being simultaneously too narrow and too broad in scope; all illegal acts are not necessarily corrupt and all corrupt acts are not necessarily illegal.' The legal focus is usually centred on bribes and embezzlement, kickbacks or the like, being limited to that which is listed in the legislation itself, which is an aspect that is highlighted in the corruption legislation developed over the years. One example is the EU legal framework that specifically points to the duties of EU public officials, describing in detail their roles – detailing what is permitted and what is not, effectively delimiting the public official's role and responsibilities through explicit descriptions which positively give a framework to operate within but is limiting just for the same reasons.

The problem with this legal type of definition is that it excludes many forms of what others may define as corruption, such as various types of favours and systematic types of favouritism to specific groups in which money is not involved. This can take the form of jobs in the public sector, various permits for business or construction or access to public services that are in high demand but 'rationed'.

Some of the earliest legislation specifically aimed at corruption is to be found in three English statutes – the Public Bodies Corrupt Practices Act of 1889, the Prevention of Corruption Act of 1906 and the Prevention of Corruption Act of 1916. These acts define corruption to include three main ingredients, where the central focus is upon the narrow 'gift or consideration' in relation to 'public bodies and government departments' (Hodgkinson 1997, p. 18). Here corruption's main three ingredients are (1) that a gift of consideration was given or offered by one party to another, (2) that the gift or consideration was given, or received, as an inducement or reward for services to be rendered or already rendered in relation to official duties and (3) that the transaction took place corruptly (Salmon 1976, 18). The statutes, however, are broader than early twentieth-century legislation surrounding corruption, a result stemming from the legislation placing the onus upon both corrupter and corruptee – allowing a broad scope of application. The listing of the 'main ingredients' of corruption provides the narrow focus, whereas the mention of actors to whom it applies instantly broadens the scope of the legislation.

An example of the early legislation from the twentieth century (and perhaps the narrowest) is the American Foreign Corrupt Practices Act (FCPA) of 1977. An example of the narrow focus of the legislation is its stipulation of 'payment of money or anything of value' as part of the acts considered to be corrupt covered by the law. The FCPA came about as a direct result of the Watergate scandal, when the US political image across the globe was seen as weak, especially as political corruption of the highest order was taking place within its own borders. Apart from serving as a grace-saving device, this legislation was to serve as a tool to stymie the 'additional costs' that American businesses were incurring in the payment of bribes in their dealings overseas. However, the scope of the legislation was to be limited to the dealings of the private sector and its actors – businesspeople, companies and corporations – leaving the public sector and its employees out of its ambit. Although the modern legislation surrounding corruption was initiated by the private sector, it slowly transitioned to a broader scale to include the public sector/public officials.

Similar formulations make up the Organisation for Economic Co-operation and Development (OECD) Anti-Bribery Convention. However, the scope is broadened in this convention by including 'other advantages', leaving room for interpretation of whether the advantage is pecuniary or not.[2] These two acts target the supply side of the corruption exchange; however, the development of the corruption legislation of the 1990s (e.g. the European Council Criminal and Civil Law Conventions on Corruption) kept broadening the coverage not only in terms of the definition of 'corruption' but also in terms of expanding the coverage to both the supply and demand sides.

An aspect that has received a lot of criticism is the fact that the United Nations Convention against Corruption (UNCAC), established in 2003, does not define 'corruption', whereas 'public official' is defined and delimited. It can be argued that the potential absence of one is to allow leeway for the legislation to cover situations of nepotism, patronage and patrimonialism. On the other end, extremely broad definitions of both corruption and corrupt conduct in legislation can be found as well. An apt example in this case is the Australian Independent Commission Against Corruption Act of 1988, which sets out what is meant by corruption in Section 8 of the act, describing not only corrupt conduct that can vary from 'any conduct of any person (whether or not a public official) that adversely affects, or that could adversely affect, either directly or indirectly, the honest or impartial exercise of official functions by any public official, any group or body of public officials or any public authority'.

The scope of this act is so broad that an entire list of offences is offered that would be considered corruption. An important aspect that sets this legislation apart is that it includes within its ambit also the spheres outside public officials, effectively including citizens as equally culpable of a corrupt act when interacting with public authorities. This is in contrast to much of the other anti-corruption legislation that merely focuses on the public official's conduct. The onus is upon both

---

[2]  OECD Anti-Bribery Convention of 1997, Article 1.1: 'Each Party shall take such measures as may be necessary to establish that it is a criminal offence under its law for any person intentionally to offer, promise or give any undue pecuniary or other advantage, whether directly or through intermediaries, to a foreign public official, for that official or for a third party, in order that the official act or refrain from acting in relation to the performance of official duties, in order to obtain or retain business or other improper advantage in the conduct of international business.'

parties to behave in a non-corrupt and impartial manner, a view that fits well with our Republican understanding of corruption and that which is the 'good society'.

A further reason for the legal understanding of corruption as narrow is that the legal/illegal divide can easily exclude corrupt acts that are not covered by the law but may still be ethically wrong in the eyes of the public, such as instances of nepotism. As Kotkin and Sajó (2002, p. 3) point out, '[G]overnmental sleaze is often completely legal but still unethical, for instance, the taking of a vacation in Madagascar and claiming the trip was intended to study how that country's public administration operates.' This is an appropriate example of a case where officials act within the legal framework and where their actions would not be classed as illegal per se but would be seen as corruption by many citizens. This, we argue, is the main limitation of the legal conceptualization of corruption.

Another limitation of legalistic definitions of corruption is in the case of systems where the legal setup is such that extortion is embedded within the system and where this would be considered legal – an example of which, according to Kotkin and Sajó (2002), can be found in some post-communist countries. Although the legal definition of corruption is often viewed as the safe route to take, what is overlooked is that laws may be enacted that allow the use of public office in ways that would be seen and understood by many citizens as corruption.

## Corruption from Sociological and Anthropological Perspectives

The sociological perspective of corruption is a latecomer to the corruption debate (Hodgkinson 1997, p. 17); however, it is one that makes an important contribution. Unlike the prevalent liberal approach (where the focus has remained upon the individual, i.e., the public official), the sociological aspect investigates the state–people linkage, veering focus away from the individual, raising it to the organizational level and effectively bringing into focus the society at large. At the centre of the sociological approach is the evolving character of the state–society relation, which is looked at to understand *how* corruption is operating, wherein the individual finds himself or herself. This approach redirects attention to the organizational behaviour and organizational rationality, which is an advantage because it takes into account the evolving character of corruption in association with the evolving character of the state (as an organization). Renowned Malaysian sociologist Syed Hussain Alatas's (1968) model of corruption helps us to gain an overview of this nuanced approach:

1. a betrayal of trust;
2. deception of a public body, private institution, or society at large;
3. deliberate subordination of common interests to specific interests;
4. secrecy of execution ... ;
5. the involvement of more than one person or party;
6. the presence of mutual obligations and benefits, in pecuniary or other form;
7. the focusing of attention on those who want definite decisions and those who can
8. influence them;
9. the attempt to camouflage the corrupt act by some form of lawful justification;
10. the expression of contradictory dual functions by those committing the acts.

This involves important nuances that can be detected by characteristics (2) and (3), where the collective is weighed in heavily versus the individual. This aspect, where the changing character of the organization is taken into account, is one that remains overlooked within current corruption research, resulting in the non-detection of the presence of corruption within developed countries, where a 'primary' understanding of corruption is still used, such as those found in economic understandings (e.g. 'bribes' and 'kickbacks').

In one of the earliest expositions on corruption, Alatas ventures to systematically explore and theorize the concept itself, wherein the focus remains on the holistic level of the effect of corruption at all possible levels of the state, whether this be 'economic, administrative, political or judicial realms' (Alatas 1999, p. 13). This approach is expounded through viewing corruption as three different stages of evolution. We are presented with these stages as a thermometer of the damage caused to society at large.

The first stage is that where corruption is relatively limited, taking place (in and by) the elite of society without affecting the wider area of social life, or as Montesquieu emphasized, '[C]orruption always begins with gentleman' (Rotberg 2016, p. 453). This involves the upper echelons of the state and big businesses, where the common people are still able to get their rights and access to government without having to resort to corrupt means, such as paying bribes. In essence, the common person is left unfettered by the corruption that is taking place in the highest strata of the state and private sector.

The second stage is when corruption is rampant – where it is all-pervading, through all sectors and classes of society, and everyone is affected, from the top to the bottom of society. Basically, a citizen cannot get around to carry out any task, whether this be registering the birth of a child, gaining a building permit to build one's home or even something as insignificant as crossing the traffic light, without resorting to corrupt means. It is the stage where one has to bribe one's way to their rights as a citizen, such as accessing healthcare, education or even law enforcement. The final stage, as well as most interesting, is where corruption itself becomes self-destructive, what Alatas labels as 'tidal corruption.' This final stage is where

[c]orruption stimulates further development of greater corruption, and this further degree in turn causes an even greater increase in corruption. When extortion becomes widespread in the civil service, and is used by policemen on the beat, the clerk at the counter, the nurse at the hospital, it is usually the effect of previous corruption at a higher level. (Alatas 1999, p. 19)

This nuanced approach to corruption analyzes and understands corruption from an aspect that is analogous to the Chinese proverb, 'The fish rots from the head down.' This proverb is instructive in the way the sociologist understands the phenomenon, in this case, the spread of corruption is from top to bottom of society, where the initial stage is found within the circles of society (the top echelons or, rather, the elite). At this stage it is not affecting the rights of the members of the elite nor those of the common people. But from here it carries down to the lower rungs of society, infecting more and more sectors and classes, where eventually the corruption is so prevalent that the one to be affected is the common person on the street. In this understanding of corruption, the concept is reiterated with a constant focus on the state officials who exercise public power (the bureaucrats, the civil servants, etc.) versus the effect on citizens, that is, the receivers of the public services provided by the state.

In contrast to the 'primary' understanding, the nature of corruption has altered due to alteration of the state and its functions wherein it exists. An important analysis of this is presented by Hodgkinson

(1997), who investigates corruption at the state level in relation to the so-called new public management reforms that have been instilled in the United Kingdom and some other Western countries.

In addition to the sociological perspective, there is also important work on corruption carried out by anthropologists (Jordan Smith 2007; Torsello 2011; Torsello and Vernand 2016). Here the focus is on understanding how people 'make sense' of corrupt practices when they are on both the receiving and the exploited ends of these exchanges. On the one hand, an ethnographic approach adds important dimensions to our understanding of how people may take a clear moral stand against corruption while at the same time participating in corrupt practices because they perceive that they have no other alternative (Rothstein and Torsello 2014; Sneath 2006; Werner 2000). On the other hand, anthropological researchers have for the most part been guided by a 'strong cultural relativism' which has 'led anthropologists to reject a moral judgment of corruption' (Torsello and Vernand 2016, p. 37). The way ethnographic research is usually conducted – that is, through a direct interaction with the observed community – opens up a number of questions and dilemmas concerning the ethical conduct of the ethnographic researcher. As stated in one anthropological study on corruption, 'Anthropology's emphasis on local rationalities and cultural logics, and the largely sympathetic sensibility of anthropologists regarding their subjects, may produce a disinclination to attach a seemingly derogatory Western label like corruption to the behavior of non-Western people' (Smith 2007, p. 10; cf. Shore and Haller 2005, p. 7) While many anthropologists have encountered various forms of corruption when doing field research, they have often hesitated to write about it for a number of reasons. One is, of course, a desire to return to the local society they have been studying, which could become problematic if the researcher is seen as condemning a central part of the behaviour of the group (Shore and Haller 2005). A second reason seems to be an effect of the ethical codes of the profession. As Torsello (2015, p. 163) writes:

The two largest professional associations in cultural anthropology (American Anthropological Association) and in social anthropology (European Association of Social Anthropologists) have clarified the deontological conditions under which fieldwork research needs to be undertaken. One of the most important points of these conditions concerns the need to avoid exposing persons who inform the researcher to any form of damage, loss or accusation because of the fieldwork data. Anthropologists are under a paradoxical injunction regarding fieldwork leading to the discovery of corrupted practices. On the one hand, one goal of anthropology is to carry out in-depth qualitative analyses to reveal the details of this illicit phenomenon. On the other hand, the ethnographer cannot put into danger the people under observation.

Owing to the delicate nature of corruption as a topic of investigation, reporting instances of corruption as observed by the anthropologist may of course result in a clear and direct violation of the established ethical codes. The result is that ethnographers' accounts of corruption often seem quite disappointing for those who would like to read first-hand local descriptions of how people in various types of local societies handle and view corruption. It goes without saying that corruption is a complex phenomenon which, in everyday practices reported in ethnographic research, is inextricably linked to a number of other forms of social interactions, such as, for instance, gifts, reciprocity, friendship, kin ties, patronage, identity, affection and even love.[3] Anthropologists, who have traditionally carried out ethnographic research on most of these themes are likely to have discovered corruption more by chance than by directly searching for it. Moreover, the ethnographic approach focusing on corruption per se brings about a number of epistemic questions concerning the ethnographer's authority, the fact of taking a moral standpoint in judging the observed practices, as well as the confrontation between the ethnographer and the studied socio-cultural differences.

The unwillingness to take a moral stand about corrupt practices, the intention to return to the local society from which data have been collected, a fear of being accused of ethnocentrism and the maybe unforeseen effects of the ethical codes of the profession have affected the usefulness of the anthropological approach. Nevertheless, our interpretation of parts of this research is that much of it is in line with the 'collective action' approach to corruption as presented by Persson et al. (2013). A 'culture of corruption' as expressed by, for example, Jordan Smith (2007) does not imply that corrupt practices are ingrained in the culture and seen as normatively acceptable by people even in systemically corrupt societies. Instead, we interpret

---

[3] For a detailed exposition of 'the gift', see Alatas (1999, pp. 28–33), where he refutes the Western interpretation of gift giving as corruption on the premise that intentions and sensibilities of what constitutes an acceptable form of a gift tends to be a norm within the society of which both receiver and giver are aware.

much of the findings about corruption from anthropology as an effect of how people living under dysfunctional and corrupt public institutions are forced to act in ways that contribute to the continuation of corruption, although they do not internalize corrupt practices as morally acceptable (for an overview of this literature, see Rothstein and Torsello 2014).

# 3 | *The Evolution of Corruption as a Concept*

The concept of corruption is an age-old issue, perhaps as old as human civilization (Alatas 1999; Jordan 2009; Mulgan 2012; Von Alemann 2004). The underlying meaning of the concept that is understood universally, no matter what culture or society, is the one forwarded by religion – where morality and corruption are two sides of the same coin (or two binary products of human interaction). The soul represents purity, while sin represents the immoral act, which effectively corrupts the soul.

Maybe the most prominent example from the Abrahamic religions is that of Adam eating the apple in the Garden of Eden, giving in to the temptation that was forbidden to him. Or to use one of the nine definitions found in the *Oxford English Dictionary*, 'Moral (corruption) – a making or becoming of morally corrupt; the fact or condition of being corrupt; moral deterioration or decay; depravity' (from Heidenheimer et al. 1989, p. 7).

The biblical origins of the concept were briefly alluded to by Carl Friedrich when he analyzed the moral and political paradox forwarded by Lord Acton in his famous dictum 'power tends to corrupt and absolute power corrupts absolutely':

> Such deep suspicion of power has, it would seem, a religious root, and is typically Western and Christian. It harks back to the notion of the kingdoms and to the contrast between the earthly and the heavenly city ... Such corruption, being in fact a decomposition of the body politic through moral decay, is a general category to include all kinds of practices which are believed to be dysfunctional and hence morally corrupt. (Freidrich 1972, p. 16)

The role played by the Augustinian tradition in the moral and political conception of corruption is further reflected in an argument made by Génaux (2004). In tracing the evolution of the term 'corruption' within the social sciences, she argues that 'corruption did not belong to the legal vocabulary of the Ancient Regime but to a politico-moral lexical field mainly drawn from the Bible ... "Corruptio" and "corruption" are in effect biblical words whose function is central to the Holy Book' (Génaux 2004). It is this moral lens through which corruption has been analyzed in the political thought ranging from Enlightenment thinkers to contemporary scholars. Some have traced the roots of the concept of corruption within social settings as far back as to antiquity. Scholars such as Noonan trace the roots of the concept to the Middle East, where in Mesopotamia and Egypt 'from the fifteenth century B.C. on, there has been a concept that could be rendered in English as "bribe", of a gift that perverts judgment' (Noonan 1984, p. 13; cf. Chayers 2015). Noonan demonstrates how corruption as a notion has been present since antiquity and been under debate in Greece (and then Rome) since the days of Aristotle.

The politico-moral character of corruption has remained a constant throughout its conceptual evolution. This is evidenced by the way the Romans used it 'in reference to a specific human activity (bribery) or in the more general sense of destroy, lay waste, adulterate or spoil' (Euben 1989, p. 220). Both moral and political terms are the basis for understanding corruption. An example of this is the Roman usage of corruption to cover 'political decline'. Furthermore, Génaux highlights the presence of corruption as a concept within Roman law:

[I]n law the term had ... an official status associated to the criminality of certain agents of public power: 'corruption' was used in Roman law as in ius commune to incriminate the practices inherent to the exercise of justice. (Génaux 2004)

This quotation highlights the fact that the term 'corruption' was very much within the public realm in the Roman republic, where the term was applicable to holders of public power. This further highlights the link between the understanding of corruption and what is considered as justice, where a holder of public power who is responsible for exercising justice is considered corrupt if he fails to deliver this. According to this line of thought, an unjust power holder is corrupt; ergo, corruption is injustice.

Parallel to the Roman understanding of corruption is that found in the Islamic world. In contrast to the Roman usage, the Islamic authorities from the eleventh century, such as the famous Hanafite law manual *Mukhtasar al-Quduri*, discuss different categories of bribes, providing evidence of the presence of the concept of corruption within the legal codes from a very early stage. Not only was corruption part of the legal codification, but the negative effects and dangers of corruption on governance, and the health of the state itself, also were eminently felt and discussed:

Now there's a risk of disruption to the existing order if men persist in nullifying the true and regularising the false. The judges of Islam and sultans in the past, in order to prevent that danger and to eliminate the potential causes of the state's decay, shut tight the door of bribery, transacted their business in accordance with the law, and kept their people under the law too. (Çelebi 1957, p. 127)

The recognition of the dangers of corruption to include a 'state's decay' is blatant – for which a suggested remedy offered is the legal code, alongside pointing out the need for tight regulation around briber as well as respect for the laws. From the existing authorities we can gather that the concept was very much in the legal codes as well as within the ruler's understandings of what dangers governance faces. In addition, what stands out as insightful in this early writing is the recognition of the limitations of legal codes and codifications. 'It is no use saying "We have employed a legal device"; there are many actions which can be dressed in the garb of legality but are not acceptable to the reason, because of the manifold corruptions lurking beneath' (Çelebi 1957, p. 127). This is reminiscent of the earlier discussion of corruption's classification as legal/illegal and the limitations surrounding this.

In recognition of the limitations of legal codification, the focus instead is directed at the importance of *implementation* (i.e. the exercise, the output side of the equation) of these laws. The quotation poignantly highlights that all corruption is not necessarily illegal, or covered by law; it is at times 'dressed in the garb of legality', reminding us that the concept of corruption is not limited to what is 'technically' seen as legal. Instead, the politico-moral importance of the concept is reinforced.

This early Islamic understanding of corruption, however, takes the consideration and analysis of corruption a step further by debating and discussing where the onus of responsibility lies – that is, whether it is the receiver or the giver of the bribe that is in the wrong and should be punished or if it is both receiver and giver of bribes that are to be held responsible. Although the references pertain to bribes, the exercise of extrapolation of concepts can be assumed to be present from the practice of *qiyas* (use of analogy) as well as the writings of various Muslim scholars. One in particular, writing in the seventeenth century, the Ottoman scholar Kâtip Çelebi, analyzes these various authorities in a brief chapter on bribery found in his treatise, *The Balance of Truth*.[1] He classifies bribes into two categories:

1. That which was forbidden for both parties, and
2. That which was forbidden to one party – namely, the receiver. The latter was approved if the intention was to avoid harm.

The strength of this categorization is enhanced when put into the context of public and private spheres – that is, the citizen and the state. The first type of corruption is classified as forbidden for both parties, both giver and receiver – where the onus is on both parties, effectively holding both the citizen who offers the bribe and the state representative culpable. The equal distribution effectively holds both the citizen and the state servant responsible for creating and maintaining that which is the 'good society'. Holding the same context as a constant, the second category is of special interest because here the heavier onus is put upon the public servant by forbidding the corruption of this agent as the receiver. This underpins the relative importance of a state servant's position, where their role significantly affects the whole of society versus that of the individual citizen's action. The citizen is by no means absolved of responsibility for his or her actions, but the role and moral responsibility of the citizen are placed in the background. The striking feature of the second category is the exception that is forwarded – that is where the bribe/corruption is 'approved' as long as the intention of receiving the said bribe is to avoid harm. At first glance it may seem redundant; however, this important aspect highlights *why* the citizen can be without responsibility. Let us take the well-known example of a prison guard in a Nazi concentration camp. A prisoner tries to escape by offering the guard a bribe, and the guard decides to take the bribe and let the prisoner go free, knowing full well that unless he does so, the prisoner most certainly will be killed. The latter's intention in accepting the bribe is 'to avoid harm' to the prisoner, and the giving of the bribe is only instigated due to the state of

---

[1]  The authorities range from the legal manuals to open debates by the then scholars who were both public figures and also experts of jurisprudence (Çelebi 1957, p. 127).

not being able to provide justice to its citizens. This line of thought indicates that the concept of corruption is not specifically Western nor new but also reinforces the concept as very much universal and not limited to the modern liberal West (Alatas 1999; Kurer 2005; Rothstein and Torsello 2014).

The classic conception of corruption as a general disease of the body politic was also central to the thinking of Enlightenment thinkers such as Machiavelli, Montesquieu and Rousseau, aptly described by Friedrich in mapping the historical evolution of the concept. The historical evidence points to the presence of corruption during the times of these philosophers, explaining how the concept entered the political thought through the religious venue and was seen as a moral problem and/or a problem of virtue (Freidrich 1972, p. 19).

The use of this politico-moral analysis is elaborated by Ritner (2011), who shows how Machiavelli, extrapolating from the religious realm to the political realm, conceptualized corruption as the greatest ill in government, capable of bringing down an entire state. Although Machiavelli builds upon the republican interpretation of corruption, Ritner argues that Machiavelli does not view a particular government as black or white ('good' or 'bad') but as moving on a scale of different shades of grey with the main focus on maintaining an enduring state (Ritner 2011). In a similar manner, Heidenheimer (2002) traces the understanding of corruption back to the fathers of Western classical political thought – Aristotle and Plato.

## Republicanism versus Liberalism

This tracing process, mentioned earlier, brings to our attention the republican school of political philosophy through which Aristotle and Plato understood corruption. Before embarking on the contrast between liberalism and republicanism, it is imperative to distinguish the republicanism to which we refer. In the literature, there are two stark strands of republican political theory: on the one hand, the contemporary understanding of virtue and liberty in relation to the *individual* and, on the other hand, the classical republicanism that focuses on virtue and liberty in relation to the *collective*. This is traced back to different periods where the former relates to Cicero and the Roman understanding of republicanism, which came about due to private property laws. It is from this republican tradition that Machiavelli's understanding of this problem is said to stem (Dryzek et al. 2006). On the other hand is the Greek or Aristotelian type of republicanism that also focuses on virtue and liberty but with the collective as its fulcrum. For a brief understanding of what this classical republicanism is, we will turn to the fundamental difference between liberalism and republicanism so that one may effectively differentiate the concepts and allow them to stand in their own right (Gerring 2012).

In liberal theory, society is viewed in two parts: the public/collective (that which is seen as outside, cold and distant from oneself) and the private (inside, close to oneself and familiar) (Pitkin 1981) and where the private trumps the public. There is a clear distinction and existence of the two entities 'private' and 'public.' As is evident from Hobbes' writing, there is a separation of the two, where only one survives, without the other, effectively dissipating the need to focus upon the tension that is created between the two realms. This results in leaving out any analysis or discussion of the overlap that exists between the two. The main concern in liberalism is the individual because the 'I' is always trumping the 'we'.

In contrast, the classical republican school does not adhere to this separation of 'I' and 'we' but views society as a whole, taking into account both the public (collective) and the private (individual) simultaneously, where the collective (public) is viewed as superior in relation to the individual (private), entirely flipping the outlook of how the world is viewed – that is, with the collective at centre stage. It is this holistic approach that accepts the tension that exists between all aspects of pairs of values, one of which is the collective value versus the individual, echoing the need for a balancing act in order to reach the public values constituting the 'good society'.

The classical republican outlook gives weight to both 'we' and 'I' and thrives off the tension that is created in the duality. This focus on the collective (in classical republicanism) versus the liberal-individualistic is succinctly summarized by Aristotle's analogy to the human body:

> [T]he state is by nature clearly prior to the family and to the individual since the whole is of necessity prior to the part; for example if the whole body be destroyed, there will be no foot or hand except in an equivocal sense, as we might speak of a stone hand for when destroyed the hand will be no better . . . The proof that the state is a creation of nature and prior to the individual is that the individual, when isolated, is not self-sufficing; and therefore he is like a part in relation to the whole. (Aristotle 2000, p. 29)

It is this fundamental difference in point of departure that translates into the different conceptions that the respective schools have of what constitutes the 'good society' and man's role in society, liberty, politics and, of course, 'corruption'. In liberal thought, the role of politics in the 'good society' is to dominate others. As Shumer (1979, p. 10) points out, according to leading contemporary political scientists such as Robert Dahl, men are by nature 'privatised and ... they relate to each other in the political sphere in terms of private interests and through the medium of power as domination'. To begin with, in this liberal-individualistic approach, man is not viewed as a 'political animal', where the primary relation is to the collective 'body politics'. Instead, man is viewed as privatized, and this outlook (through the lens of private versus public) creates a trade-off where 'privately oriented men perceive the political arena only as a place to project their own interests in competition with others' (Shumer 1979, p. 9). There is a choice to be made, and in this choice, the 'self' is always primary to the collective instead of allowing both 'public' and 'private' to co-exist. In this liberal-individualistic ideology, the 'good society' is seen as a playing field of constant trade-offs and interest struggles where 'the raw capacity to dominate mediates political relationships, resulting in decisions [that] inevitably go to the most powerful whose private interests win the competition' (Shumer 1979, p. 46). This individual focus has been criticized as to how it can get out of control:

[W]hen private gain is the sole motivating force there are no checks to restrain either violence of disputes or search for complete domination. It undermines a people's political potential. For privatised politics enacts the deliberate refusal to seek for the universal or general and it is to reject even the attempt to distinguish between subjective private desire and a collectively determined public good. (Shumer 1979, p. 11)

In the alternative republican thought, the 'good society' is a collective action problem. All agents may very well know that if they just strive for their own self-interest, the famous free-rider problem will risk destroying the possibilities for creating the 'public goods' they all need to prosper (Olson 1965; Ostrom 1990). Moreover, if for some reason such public goods have been created, such as the rule of law or an impartial and honest public administration, self-interest may reach levels of individual opportunism that the goods in question will be destroyed. Distrust that 'most others' are playing fool may create a 'social trap' situation in which the agents are, by their very distrust, locked into a sub-optimal situation. This is because the necessary amount of interpersonal trust cannot simply be 'manufactured' if genuine distrust has infested the group/society, although 'everyone' knows that they would all benefit from such trust (Rothstein 2005). The genuine dilemma in all such collective action/social trap types of situations is how to balance the tension created between private self-interest and the 'public good'. This is solved through the medium of politics, helping to explain Aristotle's proclamation of man as a political animal, upon which a 'healthy society' requires its citizens to be political so that each is able to contribute to what is the overall well-being of society and thereby effectively increasing their own well-being. In her work about political representation, Hanna Pitkin reinforces the importance of citizens leading a political life because it is

the activity through which relatively large and permanent groups of people determine what they will collectively do, settle how they will live together and decide their future, to whatever extent that is within human power. Public life in this sense is of the utmost seriousness and importance. (Pitkin 1981, p. 343)

Furthermore, republican thought treats the 'good society' as something akin to a living organism, where the 'good society', along with its citizens, is also constantly changing. The values within this society are also constantly evolving and not seen as a static feature. This results in the ultimate understanding of the 'good society' as that of a balancing act between the self and the collective. As John Schaar points out, the good society is

a community in which men can be both conscious and individual and share the moral bonds and limits of the group, emphasising that the tension is important in its own right We must seek ways to live with the tension, rather than ways of abolishing either community or individual privacy. (Cited in Shumer 1979, p. 13)

This balancing act is achieved through the active participation in the political arena of a polity's citizens in which both private and public interests are allowed to exist side-by-side deciding the polity's common life. A strong criticism that the republican school is met with is that it is self-sacrificing of individual needs and identity. However, republicanism is not altruism, as Shumer is careful to point out:

[P]ublic values are not a form of selfless altruism, but rather the way in which a given society responds to this challenge [of handling the tension between private and public] ... Thus a political people value political action and their own participation as a way of relating to others and of coping with and shaping their common life. (1979, p. 14)

The role of individuals within the polity is seen as imperative where they are 'an active audience with their power gathered together and focused to resist when necessary'. In this form of republicanism, the individuals must be persuaded, not commanded (Shumer 1979, p. 17). However, in the liberal 'good society', citizens tend not to be political because they realize that 'they can advance their private interests more effectively through non-political means', such as being successful in markets or in social/private relations (Shumer 1979, p. 10). In contrast, the republican focus on the whole collective allows one to take into account the 'living' character of the polity, both the evolution of the polity balanced with the evolution of the individuals that make up the polity. A fitting example of this is provided by Aristotle himself:

Just as a living body is composed of parts which must grow proportionally if balance is to be saved, since otherwise it would be destroyed (if for example the foot of an animal were 4 cubits [1.78 m] and the rest of its body two spans [0.44 m]; the species may even change to another one if this disproportionate growth is not only quantitative but also qualitative), so a city also is composed of parts one of which often grows without being noticed, for example the mass of the poor in democracies or polities. (From Pellegrin 2012, p. 569)

In contrast to this, the liberal focus on the agents' self-interests creates an imbalance as it ignores the evolution that occurs at the polity's level that concerns how the individual should come to understand his or her 'true' interests or, to use the famous words of Alexis de Tocqueville, 'self-interest rightly understood'. The republican school views all aspects of society and life with a view to the 'whole', whether this is 'health'/'good society' or the opposite – corruption. The liberal view is the flip side of the same coin, where the individual reigns supreme, and all issues are viewed at the individual level whether they involve health, prosperity or corruption. In sum, and to generalize (maybe in the extreme), the republican approach views politics as a way of life and not as something separate from the private realm.

As mentioned earlier, the focus of 'I' versus 'we' is one that trickles into the various understandings of politics, whether this is liberty or corruption that exists in both schools of thought. In liberalism, where the focal point is the individual, liberty is also assessed at the individual level, where the tension that exists is between the individual and the political sphere (i.e. the state). In liberalism, there is a constant suspicion that the authorities (the collective) want to usurp individual liberty. Some scholars have gone so far as to criticize liberalism as not actually having a concept of what the good life constitutes. As pointed out by the communitarian philosopher Michael Sandel, '[M]y objection to liberalism is not that it emphasises individual rights but that it seeks to define and defend rights without affirming any particular conception of the good life' (Sandel 1999, p. 210).

However, republicanism understands liberty as a balancing act as well, where 'common liberty' is weighed against 'individual liberty'. Shumer is one of the scholars who focuses on pointing out Machiavelli's effort at maintaining the importance of 'public liberty' in tension with 'individual liberty':

[C]ommon liberty rests on the respect and acceptance of the liberty of all. The phrase 'common liberty' contains the senses: first, that men live and act together in a political community; second that each expresses his individuality in his political action; and third that these two conflicting factors must constantly be held in tension. (1979, p. 14)

Once again, in republicanism, it is the acceptance of the existence of both public reason and individual liberties that is seen as creating the best outcome. The tension, it is argued, brings forward the best balance that serves as the basic ideal for the 'good society'. An interesting development in the scholarship surrounding republicanism is how liberalism has penetrated its understanding. A good example is the definition of republicanism provided by the *Stanford Encyclopaedia of Philosophy*. In this, Lovett (2016) provides the reader with the contemporary definition of republicanism, to be understood as political liberty. The article divides the republican scholars into groups: scholars such as Machiavelli are characterized a representing 'classical republicans', and the contemporary scholars are labelled as 'civic republicans'. What is of interest for our discussion is that this contemporary civic republicanism draws on political liberty mainly in reference to the individual, the 'I', reiterating the liberal stance where the individual/private is of central importance.

In contrast, the scholars that explore republicanism as political liberty in reference to the collective have been neatly labelled as 'civic humanists' (such as the well-known republican Hanna Arendt). This separation effectively divorces the original understanding of republicanism, where the collective is above the individual, thereby blurring the distinction between the two political philosophies, a danger where modern republicanism is now in lieu with liberalism.

Scholars such as Dagger not only encourage this overlap but clearly aim to create a category of its own, a hybrid that focuses on the similarities of the two political theories. As he states it, '[W]e should pause to consider whether republicanism and liberalism share enough features to make a hybrid possible, perhaps in the form of a "more civic-minded liberalism" that might be called republican liberalism' (Dagger 1999, p. 210). This search for similarities between republicanism and liberalism unfortunately negates the opportunity to critically assess the flaws that exist in today's political science realms. Instead of labelling the critics as civic humanists, we argue that the scholarly realm should take heed to Shumer's (1979) advice and use this political theory to reassess the current state of affairs from the viewpoint of 'outside' eyes in order for us to improve the current political theories that we use (Shumer 1979; cf. Sandel 1999).

## Corruption through Republicanism versus Liberalism

Unlike today's liberal understanding of corruption, the republican school of thought, developed by Aristotle, explores this 'dysfunctional' character of corruption that is rooted in the relationship between politics and philosophy, *sophia* and *phronesis*, effectively a politico-moral understanding of corruption. Aristotle viewed government as a duality, as good versus bad, corruption versus virtue, and thereby as a balancing act where the state was not examined in isolation on any single matter but viewed in the context of dualities. According to Euben (1989, p. 227), Aristotle adopts a moral definition of corruption as he defines the concept in his *Politics*.

This definition – 'When a constitution systematically falls short of the paradigms of action, character, and justice which give it unity and definition, it is corrupt' – is propounded in connection to what Aristotle understood as the 'good society' or ideal regime, which will lead to the

society's ultimate goals of virtue and happiness because states ultimately exist for virtue and happiness of their citizens. It is in reference
to this idea that corruption is conceptualized and where corruption and
virtue form the basis for good/bad government, thereby creating
a duality. Therefore, in order to understand Aristotle's conception of
corruption, it is imperative to have a 'correct' understanding of what
according to him constitutes the 'good society'. According to Aristotle,
there are six main characteristics constituting a 'good society' (from
Heidenheimer et al. 1989, pp. 227–9):

1. Citizens share in the administration of justice.
2. All commercial transactions subject to moral purposes of household
   management, towards the moral ends of polis.
3. Plurality of contributions and points of view.
4. [Equality] . . . what matters is that equals be treated equally and unequals
   be treated unequally.
5. Private interests or associations subordinate to higher more inclusive
   public interests and associations.
6. Citizens are soldiers and soldiers are citizens.

As Euben points out, Aristotle was concerned about the moral quality
of public life. The very first pillar reinstates the importance of the
philosophical stance of morality, singling together morality and politics,
where effectively a 'polis' (i.e. a state) is a partnership in virtue shared
between citizens. The strand of morality in understanding the concept of
corruption is followed through in each and every pillar, where the
collective good is viewed as superior to that of the individual good,
and political action is always weighed against the virtue of the society.
This is evidenced in the second condition, where, faithful to the principle
of duality, the condition is followed by an explanation of what corruption would be: 'a corrupt city is one where gain is valued over friendship,
private interest valued over common good and materialist ideologies and
motives are the animating forces of individual and collective life' (Euben
1989, p. 228). The collective or common good ('moral ends of the polis')
is weighed above that of the private/individual – the importance of which
is highlighted by the third condition, an issue further elaborated by
Euben:

Each citizen must be committed to the common good but this needs to be
viewed through different eyes. It is the shared view that becomes the basis for
mere difference to become recognised as diversity. (Euben 1989, p. 228)

Once again, two opposite principles provide the basis for a healthy society in order to create the desired balance. On the other end, a corrupt society would be one in which there is politics without community or a community without politics. Understood through the lens of Aristotle's 'good society', corruption constitutes that which goes against the moral well-being of society, that is, a situation that ultimately contradicts the 'common good' (as decided by the collective). If, on the other hand, the moral well-being of society is ignored, where a situation arises that ultimately contradicts the common good, the end result of this is injustice. Through this duality approach, Aristotle attempts to combine the exoteric (i.e. the material) with the esoteric (i.e. whether this be argued as philosophy or religion) in the form of morality – that is, the philosophical well-being of the society when assessing how best to achieve the idea of 'good government'. Ultimately, a corruption-free society is a public good. In Aristotle's own words:

In all sciences and arts the end is a good, and especially and above all in the highest of all – this is the political science of which the good is justice, in other words, the common interest. (p. 125 in *Politics*)

In essence, the common interest not only elucidates the absence of corruption but also brings to fore the common interest, as well as the end goal of political science – to be justice. One of the prominent sociologists to maintain this republican outlook, where public and private are kept in constant balance, is Syed Hussain Alatas. In essence, he too reiterates this: a corruption free society, as a public good. However, he frames it as the main goal of the good society. In his exact words, '[T]he goal of state is to achieve a just and equitable society' (Alatas 1999, p. 39).

It is this inclusion of philosophy and politics on one plane that is missing in today's political science discussion surrounding the concept of corruption, rejected on the basis of the approach being 'moralistic and subjective' (You 2007). Euben's critique of the present discussion is that it uses the liberal approach in an attempt to 'develop a politically neutral, methodologically respectable, operationally viable definition of corruption' defending itself as objective, where 'empirical examination is certain to contribute more to an understanding of political corruption than the roundest condemnation' (Euben 1989, p. 243). Our argument is that a return to the republican understanding of the concept of corruption is necessary on the very grounds that the liberalists reject it, namely, that it is subjective and moralistic. However, it is only when the philosophical and the political science are married that a deeper and more solid understanding will be reached of what corruption truly is. By rejecting the republican understanding as 'moralistic and subjective', the liberalist approach not only reverts the focus solely to the individual, but it also distances itself from the moral foundations of the republican idea of corruption. A problematic consequence of this is that the liberalist approach ultimately distances itself from the idea of justice being a collective value – one that is decided by the society. This would be as if we were to remove the issue of human rights from the idea of intrinsic rights and instead locate them in conceptions of self-interest. As stated by Euben (1989, p. 229):

The more principles, contributions and points of view a polis includes without losing its coherence or vitiating its moral end, the more it becomes a whole, the same way that the more experience and previous thought a theory takes into account the more impartial it becomes.

As this quotation clarifies, the reason why the republican understanding of the concept of corruption needs to be brought back into the academic debate is not only to bring in 'previous thought'. Instead, the reason is to gain an understanding of what, in an increasingly globalized world, could be commonly seen as the 'good society'. As argued by Amartya Sen (2009), it is upon such shared norms of human well-being that the concept of justice must be founded, and this must ultimately be based on a set of moral arguments that are different from atomistic individuals pursuing their self-interests. The foremost example of such shared norms of human well-being are the human rights laws, which are rights intrinsic to being humans, whether or not one's state has signed up to the UN's Human Rights Declaration. The main contribution of the republican school of thought to the corruption debate is thus the insight of the complexity that surrounds the concept of corruption, where the constant balance between private and public needs to be maintained. That it is a concept that has constantly been rooted in politics, the understanding of which has evolved according to the values that we associate to our ideas of present morality and justice.

## Is a Universal Conceptualization Possible?

'The search for a robust conceptual definition of corruption is a near Sisyphean task', writes Heywood and Rose (2015, p. 103). We certainly agree and would specifically like to point at a problem faced both by academia and the policy world, namely, the conundrum of finding a balance between the universality of corruption and its relation to the environment within which it exists. It leads us to the crux of the corruption debate: is corruption a universal concept? As pointed out by the Council of Europe, '[N]o precise definition can be found which applies to all forms, types and degrees of corruption, or which would be acceptable universally as covering all acts which are considered in every jurisdiction as contributing to corruption' (Pearson 2013, p. 36). This poses many problems, one of which is bringing together the different forms of corruption such as, for example, clientelism, patronage, nepotism and patrimonialism into one comprehensive analytical concept.

Philosophically, we argue that concepts such as these all share a 'core' with corruption, which appears to be the reason justifying why these are constantly examined hand in hand (Kawata 2006; Kitschelt and Wilkinson 2007; Kotkin and Sajó 2002). It is perhaps in lieu of this that some scholars have attempted to identify a core that can be pinned down and that binds these different forms of corruption together, thereby going beyond the cultural or relativist understandings that tend to dominate within much of the empirical research. It is true that using the same concept for a situation where a policeman demands a small sum for not giving a speeding ticket and the huge sums that are reported to be paid for securing government arms deals can seem a bit awkward. However, there is a lesson to be learned from the natural sciences in this respect that alleviates this conundrum. Let us look at the example of classifications. Biologists classify humming birds, hens, eagles and ostriches all as 'birds' despite the fact that they are, to say the least, quite different 'birds'. This analogy may indicate that it is not the size of the matter that is important, but some qualitative core or aspect of the phenomenon we want to define. The purpose of the next section is to analyze the extent to which a core or a universal concept of corruption exists on a philosophical level that would connect the various forms of corruption such as clientelism, patronage, patrimonialism, particularism and state capture.

## Is There a Core to the Concept of Corruption that Is Universal?

Any attempt to analyse the concept of corruption must contend with the fact that in English and other languages the word corruption has a history of vastly different meanings and connotations.

– Heidenheimer and Johnston (2002, p. 3)

The preceding quotation suggests that corruption is seen by many as a relativistic concept where culture, history and language play a role in how the term is understood. However, such an analysis ignores the fact that corruption appears to be something that all societies shun and that it is not confined to the Western states (Alatas 1999; Rothstein and Torsello 2014). In Latin, the word is *corrumpere*, meaning 'decay', whereas, for example, in Urdu, the word for corruption is *be-imaan*, literally translating to 'without conscience'. All languages may not share the same or similar term for corruption, but the underlying concept and the general understanding are what have remained the 'red thread' within societies. This is well illustrated by Kotkin and Sajó:

Even if the code of certain societies emphasises the importance of gift-giving, including public transactions, it is clear that such gift rules do not rule out the concept of impermissible levels of gifts or a disregard of public duties. A gift culture does not exclude either the concept of public trust or the breach of rules in exchange for impermissible advantages. Furthermore, because of increased intra- and inter-societal communication and exchange, the chances of a universal understanding and condemnation of actual practices have increased. (2002, p. 30)

This highlights a truth that appears to be implicit within the research and policy circles – that there can be a universal understanding of what corruption constitutes even if all languages do not share the identical term. As Karklins (2005, p. 6) points out, there may be a difference in the way corrupt acts express themselves, but that does not change the core meaning of the concept. This point is particularly relevant to the discussion that has erupted concerning the issue if the increased anti-corruption efforts from many international organizations are to be seen as hiding a neoliberal, Western liberal or post-colonial political and ideological agenda.

The development of the international anti-corruption regime since the late 1990s has not been without its critiques. One point that has been stressed in this critique is that the international anti-corruption agenda represents a specific Western liberal ideal that is not easily applicable to countries outside that part of the world (Bracking 2007; Bratsis 2003; Bukovansky 2006; de Maria 2010; Hindess 2005; Wedel 2014). There are at least two arguments against this type of relativistic conceptual framework. The first is normative and based on the similar discussion in the areas of universal human rights and the principles of representative democracy. First, the right not to be discriminated against by public authorities, the right not to have to pay bribes for what should be free public services and the right to be treated with 'equal concern and respect' by the courts are in fact not very distant for what counts as universal human rights. For example, for people who do not get the healthcare to which they are entitled because they cannot afford the bribes the doctors demand, corruption can result in a life-threatening situation. The same can be true for citizens who do not receive protection by the police because they do not belong to the 'right' group. The second reason against a relativistic definition of corruption is empirical. Although the empirical research in this area is not entirely unambiguous, most of it points to the quite surprising result that people in very different cultures seem to have a very similar notion of what should count as corruption. Survey results from regions in India and in sub-Saharan Africa show that people in these societies take a very clear stand against corruption and view the problem in much the same manner as it is understood in, for example, Denmark or by organizations such as the World Bank and Transparency International (Afrobarometer 2006; Widmalm 2005, 2008; see also Miller et al. 2001; Nichols et al. 2004). To illustrate this, respondents to the Afrobarometer's (2006) survey in eighteen African countries were asked about their views on the following scenarios where an official 'decides to locate a development project in an area where his friends and supporters live'; 'gives a job to someone from his family who does not have adequate qualifications' and 'demands a favour or an additional payment for some service that is part of his job'. As can be seen from Figure 3.1, a clear majority of the 25,086 respondents considered all three hypothetical actions of the official to be 'wrong and punishable', while only a small minority viewed such actions as 'not wrong at all'. Furthermore, the group that deemed these actions 'wrong but understandable' is also surprisingly small.

Widmalm (2005, 2008) found similar results in a survey study of villages in India. He found that the Weberian civil servant model

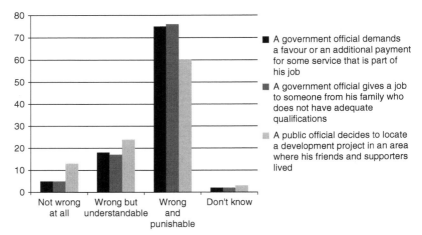

**Figure 3.1** Understandings of corruption (*n* = 25,086 for Benin, Botswana, Cape Verde, Ghana, Kenya, Lesotho, Madagascar, Malawi, Mali, Mozambique, Namibia, Nigeria, Senegal, South Africa, Tanzania, Uganda, Zambia and Zimbabwe). (Source: Afrobarometer 2006.)

(i.e. impartial treatment of citizens disregarding income, status, class, caste, gender and religion), although an absent figure in these villages, has surprisingly large support among the village population. In other words, the idea put forward by, among others, Heidenheimer (2002) as well as by most anthropologists – that the public acceptance of what is commonly understood as corruption varies significantly across cultures – does not find support in these types of studies.

The existence of a universal understanding of corruption also has been questioned among post-colonial theorists (e.g. de Maria 2010; for an overview of this literature, see Gustavson 2014). However, it can be pointed out that in Frantz Fanon's classic book, *The Wretched of the Earth*, which in many ways is ideologically the most important and founding text for the post-colonial approach to development issues, the author himself points to corruption among the new political elite as a serious malady for West Africa. In Fanon's words:

Scandals are numerous, ministers grow rich, their wives doll themselves up, the members of parliament feather their nests and there is not a soul down to the simple policeman or the customs officer who does not join in the great procession of corruption. (Fanon 1967, p. 67)

The reluctance by many scholars in the post-colonial approach to look at corruption as a serious problem for the countries they study is thus difficult to understand. In sum, there are both normative and also strong empirical grounds for opting for a universal understanding of corruption and the opposite of corruption. However, this does not exclude that there are different types of corruption and that the connection between corruption and the political system can differ. This is not different from saying that while we can have a universal definition of what constitutes representative democracy, the specific institutional configuration of democracies varies a lot. Swiss democracy is institutionally very different from the Canadian version, which, in turn, is different from what occurs in Denmark.

The reason why people, although condemning corruption, participate in corrupt practices seems to be that they understand the situation as a 'collective action' problem where it makes little sense to be 'the only one' who refrains from using or accepting bribes and other kickbacks (Karklins 2005; Mungiu-Pippidi 2015). As the Swedish economist Gunnar Myrdal stated in his analysis of the 'soft state' problem, in relation to developing countries already in the 1960s: 'Well, if everybody seems corrupt, why shouldn't I be corrupt' (Myrdal 1968, p. 409). In his anthropological study of corruption in Nigeria, Jordan Smith (2007, p. 65) concludes: '[A]lthough Nigerians recognize and condemn, in the abstract, the system of patronage that dominates the allocation of government resources, in practice people feel locked in.' In such situations, it makes little sense to be the only honest policeman in a severely corrupt police force or the only one in the village who does not pay the doctor under the table to get his or her children immunized if everyone else pays (Persson et al. 2013).

This may also be caused by a distinction pointed out by Alatas as 'extortive corruption', where people would resort to 'buying their rights'. An example of this is the need for a licence to operate a shop. It is a non-competitive and routine procedure in nature, but the government official will not issue a permit without his or her hands 'being greased'. This is as opposed to 'manipulative corruption', where one would 'deprive other people of their rights', such as paying for a job to be granted to an unqualified candidate (Alatas 1999, p. 11). This is similar to the distinction pointed out by Bauhr (2012) between 'need corruption', which she defines as paying a bribe to get a service (e.g. healthcare) to which you are legally entitled, and 'greed corruption', which is demanding a bribe for a service that you otherwise would not give even though it is your legal obligation to do so.

In his classic study of clientelism and particularism in southern Italy, Banfield (1958) found that it made perfect sense for all the families in the village of Montegranesi to be amoral familists because everyone was expected to eventually perform according to this social template. The spatial universalism of corruption increases theoretical depth when considering that even temporal approaches to this phenomenon have provided similar conclusions. Analyses of what counted as corruption in the very distant past, such as the Roman Empire, thirteenth-century France, or the fourteenth-century Islamic empire, give the impression of not being different from contemporary notions of the concept (Jordan 2009; MacMullen 1988).

The attempt to identify a core concept of corruption that can be applied universally has been present in the literature. Friedrich (1972) was one of the earliest scholars to venture onto this path, suggesting that a core meaning emerges from an overall analysis of the different meanings, offering a definition of corruption as 'a kind of behaviour which deviates from the norm actually prevalent or believed to prevail in a given context, such as the political', pointing out that what matters is private gain at public expense. The definition has been criticized as too broad, reflected also by Heidenheimer's contemplation of 'corruption' having lost meaning, so much so that replacement of the word was suggested – that was to replace it with the word 'graft' (Heidenheimer et al. 1989, p. 12). However, changing the term did not solve the problem. Instead, it was the lack of unity within the field itself as to what the concept means that resulted in the continued search for a concept that could carry that core meaning without being lost in translation. This should also highlight the importance of formulating a universal concept that refers to the core characteristics of corruption.

Another example of this is Karklins' (2005) work, in which corruption is identified as a structural problem of post-communist transition states in the form of clientelism. Karklins identifies the 'core' as 'misuse of public power for private gain', defending it to be a definition that is culturally neutral, where the underlying injustice is seen as the same everywhere (see also Sajó 2003), once again reiterating the linkages to justice that exist as an essential in all societies. In another attempt, Philip (2015, p. 22) presented what he argued is a 'core' in defining political corruption:

Corruption in politics occurs where a public official (A), violates the rules and/or norms of office, to the detriment of the interests of the public (B) (or some sub-section thereof) who is the designated beneficiary of that office, to benefit themselves and a third party (C) who rewards or otherwise incentivises A to gain access to goods or services they would not otherwise obtain.

The shortcomings of these core values are that they are only applicable in a setting where the political culture is clearly shared and there are rules governing the conduct of both public officials and members of the public in their dealings with these officials. To be more specific, because neither what should count as 'misuse of public power' nor 'the interest of the public' nor the 'norms of office' are specified, these definitions are empty shells. More specifically, we get very little information from these definitions about which norms that are transgressed when corruption can be said to occur or which norms that should be upheld by public officials in order for corruption not to occur.

Diego Gambetta (2002, p. 26) is yet another scholar who has proposed a core definition of corruption. The problem with his conceptualization is that he argues that corruption need not be unethical, inefficient or illegal. If none of these standards apply, there is, of course, no need to worry about corruption. On the other end of the spectrum are scholars such as von Alemann (2004), who regards the search for a universal concept of corruption as the academic Holy Grail, which of course means that this is something that is ultimately unattainable.

In lieu of this, von Alemann (2004, p. 26) presents a multidimensional approach that takes into account five different aspects. These are its historical development (corruption as social decline), the sociological understanding (corruption as deviant behaviour), the legal and economic perspectives (corruption as logic of exchange), corruption as a system of measureable perceptions and corruption as shadow politics. This approach argues that corruption is an ever-changing concept, which helps one to view it within its social settings, and this addresses one of the main criticisms forwarded by Alatas, which can be summarized as follows: '[P]olitical ideas are imported ready-made without any consideration as to their suitability or to the need for their adaptation to the receiving environment' specifically in the context of developing countries (Alatas 1977, p. xv). However, this ignores the core understanding that we, based on Rothstein and Torsello's anthropological analysis, argue is shared universally, that is, the underlying current for corruption being condemned in almost all known societies. The core, we argue, is the equating of corruption with some particular form of injustice.

Returning to Karklins' earlier defence of a core meaning centred around injustice, a strand of research centred on justice has developed in which the angle of injustice/justice has been taken up as the core meaning with the attempt to conceptualize corruption with a maximal definition (cf. Gerring 2012). One of the scholars who examine this maximal definition is Genaux, who forwards the proposition of the relationship between rulers and ruled (government and citizen) in every age to be centred on justice. In this relationship of ruler and ruled, the idea of justice is the main duty expected from political leaders where corruption 'started to designate the set of unjust deeds committed by the holders of supreme public offices' (Génaux 2004, p. 21). Putting forward the politico-moral angle of corruption as injustice, the term 'corruption' refers to unjust deeds committed by holders of power. Concluding that a basic core meaning of corruption does exist, that in its figurative sense has long meant, and still means, injustice, Génaux states:

In my view there does exist 'a basic core meaning' of the word and it encompasses Friedrich's definition: 'corruption', in its figurative sense, has long meant, and still means, injustice. (Génaux 2004, p. 22)

This not only reinforces why the technical sense of corruption cannot be understood without the rich polysemy of the term and also highlights the republican understanding of corruption as a collective action problem wherein a corruption-free society[2] is a public good. This is in line with the holistic perspective provided by Aristotle, in which the end good of political science (as well as that of the good society) is the common interest, specifically a society promoting virtuous behaviour.

## The Public Goods Approach

One way to understand why there seems to exist a universal understanding of what should count as corruption despite its enormous variation both in types, frequencies and locations, is what we would

---

[2] In reality, a 'corruption-free' society is as likely as a 'crime-free' society. The point is that both corruption and criminality vary a lot between different societies.

call a 'public goods approach' to this problem. In all societies/cultures, in order to survive, all groups of people have to produce at least a minimal set of public goods such as security measures, a basic infrastructure and organized/collective forms for the provision of food. As Fukuyama (2011, p. 29) has argued, the very idea proposed by rational choice–oriented contract theorists that we as humans started out as atoms in a state of nature and then decided to rationally accept a 'social contract' is highly misleading. Instead, he argues, humans were from the beginning always living in some form of societal and collective arrangements.

The very nature of a good being 'public' is that it is to be managed and distributed according to a principle that is very different from that of private goods. The public good principle implies that the goods in question should not be distributed according to the private wishes of those who are given the responsibility for managing them. When this principle for the management and distribution of public goods is broken by those entrusted with the responsibility for handling public goods, the ones who are victimized see this as malpractice and/or as corruption. This is why corruption is a concept that is related to the public and not the private sphere and why it is different from (or a special case of) theft and breaches of trust in the private sector. Corruption is usually seen as illegal, but the reason that a special term has been used for such a long time and in so many different cultures must be that it is a special form of crime different from ordinary theft.

Much of the confusion about cultural relativism in the discussion – about what should count as corruption – stems from the issue that what should count as 'public goods' differs between different societies and cultures. For example, in an absolutist feudal country where the understanding may be that the central administration is the private property of the lord/king, the state is not seen as a public good. However, in many indigenous societies with non-state political systems, local communities have usually produced some form of public goods, for example, what Ostrom (1990) defined as 'common pool resources', which are natural resources that are used by members of the group but which risk depletion if overused. Such resources are constantly faced with a 'tragedy of the commons' problem and thus are in need of public goods in the form of effective regulations to prevent overuse leading to depletion.

Our argument departs from the idea that it is difficult to envision a society without some public goods. Even a small tribe has to produce some minimal public goods such a security, handling of internal conflicts and maybe taking care of orphans. The point is: when these public goods are handled or converted into private goods, this is generally understood as corruption independent of the culture. A conclusion that follows is that we should not expect people in developing countries, whether indigenous or not, to have a moral or ethical understanding of corrupt practice that differs from, for example, what is the dominant view in Western organizations such as Transparency International and the World Bank or as that stated in the United Nations Convention against Corruption. Instead, what may differ is what is understood to fall within the public goods category.

An example could be the case in which there is not a system for taxation, but still there are certain individuals who have been selected to perform functions as arbitrators or judges. These functions are to be understood as public goods because they make it possible to solve disputes between village members/families in a non-violent way. These arbitrators may, in several cases, receive gifts from the parties involved for their services. Such gifts may, for a Westerner, look like bribes, and many anthropologists have seen them as such (Torsello and Vernand 2016). However, such gifts are usually not seen as bribes by the agents, who, in general, can make a functional distinction between bribes and gifts (Alatas 1999; Sneath 2006; Werner 2000). This implies that the gift is to be seen as a fee for a service, not a bribe. It would only be a bribe, and seen as such by the local populace, if it was given in a way to influence adjudication by favouring one party over another. In this case, the public good is converted into a private one, and it is this that is perceived as corruption. To support this argument, Rothstein and Torsello (2014) have used data from the Human Relations Area Files (HRAF) database, which is the single most comprehensive and largest ethnographic database of world cultures. The HRAF database was compiled by Yale University and includes data on 258 world cultures and over 600,000 pages of ethnographic descriptions made by professional anthropologists. The cultures covered are divided among eight world regions (i.e. Africa, Asia, Europe, Middle America and the Caribbean, Middle East, North America, Oceania and South America). Analysis of the data shows that the word 'bribe' is found in 113 of the 258 cultures, which is 48 per cent of the whole HRAF sample, excluding European countries. It is also found in all four general types of societies (i.e. foragers, horticulturalists, pastoralists and agriculturalists). The agriculturalists societies/cultures (which are also monetized and commercial) contain the largest number of bribery entries, which supports the thesis that corruption is widespread where public and private arrangements for the use of and access to resources and goods can be expected to vary. Even more interesting is the finding that pastoralist societies are apparently the least exposed to corruption among the subsistence types. This also supports the 'public goods' theory because it is in this economic type of society that one should expect to find the least ambiguity between private goods (herds and land) and public goods.

## The Core Unveiled?

Carrying forward justice as the core within the framework provided by Heidenheimer's three understandings of corruption (i.e. public office, public interest and public opinion), Kurer (2005) and Rothstein and Teorell (2008) use the subjective standard of public opinion to forward the 'impartiality principle', whereby a state ought to treat equally those who deserve equality. In order to further elaborate on the proposition of corruption as partiality (effectively injustice), it is important to first set out what the impartiality principle entails. As stated by Brian Barry, 'A theory of justice cannot simply be a theory about what justice demands in this particular society but must be a theory of what justice is in any society' (1995, p. 6). In a similar vein, the core idea of corruption in one society relates to the core idea of corruption in any society. As indicated earlier, there is a strand of literature that links corruption to injustice (Kurer 2005).

Unlike Kurer, a more direct linkage of corruption to injustice has been made by You (2015) in relation to corruption as a normative theory. Accordingly, if impartiality is justice, then corruption (i.e. partiality or favouritism) must be injustice. The opposite of justice cannot be just equality or equal treatment because in many cases we accept inequalities and unequal treatment as fair. For example, a child with learning difficulties will need more time and attention from teachers than other children. Instead, as argued by Robert Goodin, '[T]he opposite to justice is favouritism' (2004, p. 100). This would translate into a universal understanding of corruption as favouritism in the exercise of public power and equating impartiality in the exercise of public power as the special type of injustice that is the opposite of corruption. This is, in principle, a conceptualization of corruption that is applicable to any society, thereby removing it from cultural/relativistic arguments and reinforcing its universality.

In order to support our contention that a universal conceptualization of corruption is possible if it is based on the idea of injustice and favouritism, we will make use of a distinctively non-Western treatise of justice, namely, *The Muqqadimah*. This famous work, written in 1377 by the Muslim Arab (Tunisian) historian Ibn Khaldun, deals with, among many other things, Islamic political theory. In *The Muqqadimah*, 'justice' is defined as 'a balance setup among mankind' (Ibn Khaldun 1958, p. 103). To understand what *The Muqaddima* means by such a 'balanced' justice, it is necessary to look at how injustices are described. The list of examples provided is extensive, but what is interesting from our perspective is that the list comes together with a general warning against a limited understanding of injustice. For example, Ibn Khaldun warns against limiting the understanding of injustice to matters of a pecuniary nature, such as 'to imply only the confiscation of money or other property from the owners without compensation and without course' (1958, p. 107). This recognition of the dangers posed by limiting understandings of injustice lifts the concept of injustice from the particular to an attempt at a universal understanding. Of the examples provided as injustice, the most important examples provided, for our purpose, are three in particular that highlight the existence of a core understanding of corruption.

The first example of what is understood as injustice in this work is that 'people who collect unjustified taxes commit an injustice.' Bribes demanded by civil servants are exactly this, an 'unjustified tax', because it has to be paid for a public service that is already paid for by the 'justified' taxes. Public servants are adding their own 'taxes', which are unjustified, effectively mitigating the essential rights of citizens to access the service in question. The second example presented by Ibn Khaldun pertains to the *actors*; that is, 'those who deny people their rights commit an injustice' (Ibn Khaldun 1958, p. 107). Moreover, 'injustice can be committed only by persons who cannot be touched, only by persons who have power and authority.' Ibn Khaldun further states that in order to have the potential to commit an injustice, the 'person has [to have] a free hand', implying the necessity of discretion.

We can apply these two examples in our present context by looking at simple examples of civil servants providing basic rights/services in society, such as nurses, postal workers, doctors and even police officers. All these professionals have the power to withhold their specializations from citizens; nurses can withhold a treatment that a doctor has prescribed to a patient, and postal workers can choose not to send your letter or sell you a postage stamp until you have paid a little sum to them or done them a favour. All these examples involve people in positions of 'discretion' and the ability to 'deny people their rights'.

The third example relates to an understanding of corruption as a moral decay that spreads in the form of a 'social cancer' driven by greed and the perception of what others in the same situation are doing. According to Ibn Khaldun:

One person after another becomes reduced in circumstances and indigent ... Corruption of the individual inhabitants is the result of painful and trying efforts to satisfy the needs cause by their (luxury) customs; (the result) of the bad qualities they have acquired in the process of obtaining (those needs); and of the damage the soul suffers after it has obtained them, through acquiring (still) another (bad luxury) quality. (1958, p. 293)

Ibn Khaldun also makes clear that corruption is not confined to the less esteemed segments of society. Instead, he points out:

The person who is strongly coloured by any kind of vice and whose character is corrupted is not helped by his good descent or fine origin. Thus, one finds that many descendants of great families, men of highly esteemed origin, members of the dynasty, get into deep water ... because their character is corrupt ... If this (situation) spreads in a town or a nation, God permits it to be ruined and destroyed. (Ibn Khaldun 1958, p. 287)

Thus, in the *Muqqadimah*, written in the fourteenth century in the Arab Muslim world, we see traces of three contemporary general understandings what is the core of corruption, namely, bribes as unjustified taxation, injustice in the form of denial of rights, and moral decay 'from above' leading to ruin for the whole society.

One may ask what set of non-discrimination norms currently exists. The most well-established non-discrimination norms that currently exist are found in the United Nations Universal Declaration of Human Rights, and it is to these norms that we now turn.

# 4 | Corruption and Human Rights

In the preceding chapters we have mapped and analyzed how corruption has been viewed in various academic disciplines and traced the evolution of the concept itself. In tracing the concept's evolution, a discussion surrounding the universality of the concept was embarked upon, as well as a brief discussion of what constitutes the very core of corruption that transcends academic disciplines as well as geographical boundaries, helping to shed light on the overlaps that exist between disciplines pertaining to the concept. Our reiterations thus far point us in the direction of an underlying understanding of corruption and its opposite to centre on injustice/justice. In short, we have first presented what is already present in academia and briefly the policy world, followed by our own fleshing out of what we believe this core to be.

As mentioned in Chapter 1, one of the 'black holes' within existing research about corruption and quality of government is the lack of research surrounding the nexus of the anti-corruption and human rights discourses. The purpose of this chapter is to respond to the need pointed out by scholars such as Alatas (1977, 1999) and Pearson (2013) of approaching corruption from a more 'holistic' perspective that focuses its impact at the societal level instead of confining the problem to the economic and political spheres. This approach emphasizes instead the costs in overall human well-being. In the chapters that follow we will discuss the logical turn that academia can take in exploring corruption and its core understanding as injustice both within academia and in the policy realms to the other concept that has a similar core, where corruption, or rather the public good of a corruption-free society, is balanced against the highest order of private/individual rights, that is, the human rights concept. This implies relating corruption to some type of core understanding of justice and tying this in with the prevalent framework dealing with the same undercurrent theme in the policy world, thereby effectively tying in the concept within the framework of human rights.

We want to make clear that our ambition is not to develop a new corruption-centred approach to human rights. Instead, what we intend to do is to link corruption (and especially anti-corruption policies) and human rights by carrying out a more thorough normative analysis of the two discourses in tandem, propounding that which intrinsically links the two concepts, that is, the common ground that they share – whether we label this 'justice' or 'non-discrimination'.

In this chapter we will first present an overview of the current state of the research surrounding the corruption and human rights nexus. Secondly, we will specify the gap between these discourses, followed by a brief sketch of how the two discourses can be linked. Our hope is that this will result in a more intuitive linkage of the anti-corruption and human rights discourses and help to throw light on the direction we think that corruption research can take and develop itself in order to remain relevant.

Although explicit investigations of the corruption and human rights nexus remain scant, there still exists an implicit undercurrent between the two research strands at different levels, ranging from legal instruments to forms of policy output as well as the civil society movements that are active in the two spheres. The most apparent mention of a nexus that connects corruption to human rights is found within some of the legal instruments, especially within their preambles, where the linkage is expressed via the effect one has on the other. A good example of this is the EU Criminal Law Convention on Corruption, which states: '[C]orruption threatens the rule of law, democracy and human rights, undermines good governance, fairness and social justice, distorts competition, hinders economic development and endangers the stability of democratic institutions and the moral foundations of society.'

Furthermore, the implicit linkages between the two fields can also be found within the rhetoric of the different civil society movements that are active in these two fields, as well as through the common ideological ground shared by them. There are also instances where the two have run in parallel (Koechlin and Carmona 2009, p. 235). Although implicit, the linkages between these two political discourses are intuitively and empirically plausible. One example is the empirical observation that in countries where there is widespread corruption, we are likely to find more human rights violations. This intuitive and inverse relationship is also pointed out by Koechlin and Carmona: '[I]t is intuitively and empirically plausible that there is a significant correlation between low levels of corruption, human rights abuses, and the spread of corruption' (2009, p. 310). This close relationship between the two strands of research and activism is poignantly phrased by Rajagopal, calling human rights the 'sibling of the corruption discourse' (1999, p. 9).

Much of the contemporary scholarship that explores the nexus of corruption and human rights has been limited to scholars within the field of law and international law, alongside the policy world, which translated this into various policy documents produced by Transparency International as well as the International Council on Human Rights Policy (Carmona 2009; Gathi 2009; Pearson 2013; Rajagopal 1999; Rotberg et al. 2009). The overarching focus of this research can be grouped into three categories. In the first category, the focus is on the ultimate receiver. In practice, this means using human rights to give corruption a 'human face', which, in turn, is thought to reinforce the effect corruption has on intrinsic human rights – in short, the human cost that is at stake. Secondly, such an overarching focus serves to unpack the 'black box' of the anti-corruption–human rights connection and relate it to what we consider to be more specific parts of the human rights discourse. The third argument is that the human rights framework can serve to reinforce the anti-corruption framework and vice versa.

An overarching focus of the research linking anti-corruption and human rights has been to give anti-corruption a 'human face'. The intention is to recast anti-corruption from an economic issue to a more 'people-centred' issue, taking into account the toll that corruption takes upon the day-to-day lives of many citizens. This may become very important because this approach brings to the fore the human cost that occurs in relation to the end receivers of public services and goods. According to Rajagopal (1999), this can also create a sense of urgency within the population regarding the negative impact of corruption on their lives. This may well take some time, but it should be remembered that it took several decades for the UN Universal Declaration of Human Rights, which was enacted in 1948, to become something more than just 'a piece of paper'. It was first in the late 1970s that the human rights perspective on politics became a viable political tool against authoritarian governments, and the major results came first in the late 1980s when the Berlin Wall fell (Neier 2002). The United Nations Convention against Corruption (UNCAC) was enacted in 2003, and if it follows the same trajectory, we should expect it to become politically important as a tool for political mobilization in the 2030s and the first major results a decade later.

Put simply, citizens are subjected to paying bribes or to being part of other types of corrupt acts in order to access that which is lawfully their right, for example, access to public healthcare and public education. Education, for example, is an area with extensive amounts of discretionary power for teachers, principals and admission officers, and in some societies, this has led to systemic corruption in this sector (Milovanovitch 2014). As Alatas writes: '[I]n some schools, teachers squeeze gifts out of students. The good old practice of giving flowers to the teacher has been replaced by giving her a watch, an imported pen, lipstick, and even a sari' (Alatas 1999, p. 56).

The rights to healthcare and education are understood as basic human rights, and in the preceding examples these are infringed upon by acts of corruption. Other examples that point to the underlying norms connection between the two discourses are personalized bureaucracies, situations where one's connections land one a job instead of one's merits. This understanding helps to put into perspective the statement made by Gebeye (2012, p. 18), who states that 'human beings have a basic human right to live in a corruption-free society.' This most succinctly brings into focus the human foci that both human rights and anti-corruption have taken on. However, an aspect of the human cost that is left out in the main discussion of the nexus, which gives an empirical push to the relationship of the two, is the 'brain drain' that occurs from corrupt societies as a consequence of endemic corruption (Alatas 1999). This point is one that needs to be brought to the foreground of discussions in order to understand the skewed divisions that take place globally.

This human focus can also be seen in the manner in which the nexus of corruption and human rights is explored, where scholars have investigated the issue from the collective (state) level to the individual (micro) level. One advantage of focusing on the individual is the space created to unpack human rights from the broader concepts of democracy and narrow it down to specific human rights, allowing an approach that can measure both concepts empirically. This moves the discussion beyond large generalizations and engages in specifications relevant to individual citizens that link specific rights that are violated by various instances of corruption (Gathii 2009; Rotberg et al. 2009). Instead of the traditional focus on how corruption disables governments from meeting their obligations, this perspective focuses directly on how states 'respect, fulfil, and protect the human rights of [their] citizens' (Gathii 2009, p. 197).

## Relating the Legal Codes

Understanding the human rights and anti-corruption nexus in terms of human well-being can be traced back to research that investigated how corrupt acts imply that specific human rights are infringed upon (Bacio-Terracino 2008; Pearson 2013). This approach allows for a closer scrutiny of policies regarding corruption and its implications for human rights. One problem, however, is that it does not go beyond the specific legal tools and that it also leaves out the important step of relating the two at a much more basic level, where understanding of the two as symbiotic due to the normative linkage is missed.

The approaches to the linkage of human rights and anti-corruption can be more detailed and also nuanced. The first type is where human rights are seen in the order provided by the legal instruments, ranking the right that matters more if infringed by acts of corruption. The order of first-order, second-order human rights remains intact as provided by such legal instruments as the United Nations International Covenant on Civil and Political Rights and the United Nations International Covenant on Economic and Social and Cultural Rights. The rights are ranked as first order and second order (i.e. civil and political rights are treated as first-order rights, while economic, social and cultural rights are treated as second-order rights). This ordering of rights has received much academic as well as policy criticism and debate (Neier 2002). In response to this, another approach that has been used transcends this dichotomy in exchange for categorizing the covenants into approaches that concentrate on the inherent *needs* of people (Pearson 2013, p. 23). Although this analysis uses the inherent needs of people as its point of departure, the approach is a general one.

An approach that helps to enhance the empirical approach to the human rights and anti-corruption nexus is the model of analysis developed by Bacio-Terracino (2008). Firstly, the model presents a mechanism to identify whether or not a corrupt act is also to be seen as a violation of human rights. In the next step, the model helps to determine whether a corrupt act has violated a specific human right and, if so, to what extent. The model consists of three steps:

1. Identify the corrupt practice.
2. Identify the harm to the victim that affects his or her human rights.
3. Evaluate whether the corrupt practice constitutes a violation of a human right.

Through this approach, a differentiation and narrowing-down process is put in place, where the indirect and direct effects of corruption upon human rights can be separated, allowing for a clearer distinction. This also effectively removes the risk of the tautology that all corrupt acts are seen as human rights violations. This rights-based approach can help to raise awareness, allowing citizens to realize the acute danger of corruption. Bacio-Terracino (2008) argues that this transforms corruption to a much more personal issue because the corrupt action is also seen as a rights issue, and this will help to establish a zero-tolerance policy towards corruption within the population (Bacio-Terracino 2008).

Another aspect through which the human rights–anti-corruption link is explored is through their frameworks and the reinforcement one gives to the other. As Koechlin and Carmona (2009) pointed out, the frameworks of corruption and human rights are mutually reinforcing – where the human rights framework's rights-based approach is useful because its language and tools focus on codified rights as well as on discriminatory structures (cf. Chayes 2015; Rotberg 2009). The argument is that this rights-based approach can help citizens to realize the danger of corruption by making it a much more personal issue if it is also understood as violation of human rights. A human rights approach to corruption 'provides an existing international procedural framework on which to base action against corruption to achieve minimum standards of protection of rights' (Pearson 2013, p. 46). The legal instrument of the UNCAC (of 2003) presents us with a legal code indeed, but as stated earlier, it is much younger than the human rights legal instruments that have been in place since 1948. In a similar vein, the nexus also has reinforcing potential for both movements' monitoring mechanisms, where human rights monitoring could enhance the corruption monitoring framework in place, with a focus on the similarities between human rights indicators and corruption indicators (De Beco 2011, p. 1111).

On a legislative/policy level, the human rights framework is one that is well established, in contrast with the comparatively new anti-corruption legislation. An advantage connecting the two is that a human rights approach could provide an additional accountability mechanism for citizens to seek redress when their human rights have been infringed by acts of corruption, simultaneously establishing heightened awareness within states' citizens of the dangers of corruption. It no longer remains a problem belonging to 'the other' but is realized as a potent threat to the specific individual and to society as a whole.

It should be noted that the reinforcement aspect of the two research/ policy agendas of human rights and anti-corruption is not only a positive one; it can also lead to negative outcomes depending on the *way* in which human rights are argued to assist the anti-corruption or vice versa. An apt example is provided by Ghaitti (2009) in the case study of Kenya. There human rights issues are sometimes invoked as a method to circumvent corruption charges raised against individuals (in this case, prominent politicians). Paradoxically, this leads to a situation in which the human rights claims increase corruption.

## The Gap: A Normative Connection

What appears to be missing in the literature is the normative basis linking human rights and corruption discourses. By this we mean a more thorough normative analysis that would provide a philosophical and theoretical basis for the relationship. This section will attempt to trace the normative underpinnings that connect the anti-corruption and human rights norms. Firstly, we will examine the trajectories that the two have taken in establishing themselves as international norms, followed by a highlighting of the philosophical commonalities of the two discourses.

Let us first turn to the different trajectories that the human rights and anti-corruption discourses have taken in evolving into international norms. Firstly, to situate them, we argue that both can be traced back to important forms of religious teachings. In today's 'human well-being' outlook, for example, the idea of an intrinsic right to be equal in front of an almighty power stands along corruption as being the main ill one is meant to stay away from. Today the interpretations of both norms are seen as over and above the relation to any religion per se and are instead linked to the fact that human beings have intrinsic rights.

Secondly, both norms have travelled from being considered part of the private concerns of individuals to the concern of the collective society, where the norms are to be shared and valued. Thirdly, both norms initially developed as political instruments only to evolve into being viewed as societal issues so much so that a society that does not provide for basic human rights is also often flagrantly corrupt. Such states are often termed 'failing states' (cf. Acemoglu and Robinson 2012; Bates 2008).

Both concepts gained traction during the 1970s, but the concept of human rights was the one that made it to the foreground, whereas corruption as a subject matter remained, for the most part, an intellectual taboo, a situation that had much to do with the newly independent former colonies. A good example of this traction and hand-in-hand development is best captured by the example of the US administration led by Jimmy Carter, who actively pursued both of these norms (even though one caught on faster than the other). Not only was the Carter administration a big proponent of the human rights movement, but its introduction of the legal instrument of the Foreign Corrupt Practices Act (FCPA 1977) also signalled its ambition to protect and uphold both these norms on the world stage. It is probably not just a coincidence that this happened right after the Watergate scandal. The FCPA was a clear indication of honing in on the private sector by the state apparatus. The introduction and implementation of the first anti-corruption instrument in the United States, the FCPA, was mirrored by a simultaneous signing of the International Covenant on Civil and Political Rights in 1977. The human rights initiative was not confined to merely the legal sphere of the country but stood apart from the anti-corruption movement by the implantation and dissemination of the human rights agenda through a reiterating of human rights by various civil society organizations and an opening up of a new front in the Cold War to counter the Soviet Union.

On the legal front, both norms have independent trajectories in relation to the level at which they were first mobilized and then taken forward. On the one hand, the human rights norm can be seen as an example of a top-down initiation. It started at the highest level, and then it trickled down to the regional level, eventually entering the national legal frameworks of sovereign states. This is evidenced by the various treaties and legal instruments – such as the Universal Declaration of Human Rights (1948), the International Covenant on

Table 4.1 *Anti-Corruption and Human Rights*

| Anti-corruption | Human rights |
| --- | --- |
| 1977 Foreign Corrupt Practices Act | 1948 Universal Declaration of Human Rights |
| 1997 OECD Anti-Bribery Convention Inter-American Convention against Corruption | 1953 European Convention on Human Rights |
| 1999 European Union (Criminal and Civil Law Conventions on Corruption) | 1966 International Covenant on Civil and Political Rights; International Covenant on Economic, Social and Cultural Rights |
| 2003 African Union Convention on Preventing and Combating Corruption; United Nations Convention against Corruption | 1978 American Convention on Human Rights |

Civil and Political Rights (ICCPR) as well as the International Covenant on Economic, Social and Cultural Rights (ICESCR, 1966) and the European Convention on Human Rights (ECHR, 1953), followed by the adoption by all EU Member States of the ECHR, which caught on, with most countries bringing about their own national instruments in a similar fashion.

On the other hand, institutionalization of the anti-corruption norm can be seen as being more of a bottom-up process in its legal trajectory. Starting with FCPA, a private-sector lobbied initiative, constitutes the first instrument of its kind in modern law, which was later rallied to regional bodies such as the Organisation for Economic and Co-operation and Development, the European Union, and finally, the United Nations (see Table 4.1).

These two similar trajectories of the two norms have been examined and analyzed independently without linking the two. As can be seen from the preceding examples, the focal point of linkages between the human rights and anti-corruption norms has been limited to the legal/legislative linkages that exist between the two. It is interesting that this has remained the case for such a long time, even though the preambles of these legal instruments clearly point to the normative connection shared by these two legal movements. As stated above, the Preamble to the Council of Europe Convention on Corruption states: 'Corruption threatens the rule of law, democracy and human rights,' clearly delineating the relationship between corruption and human rights. An even more interesting point, however, is where the authors of the Preamble point us in the direction of the underlying normative basis upon which both anti-corruption and human rights are based, namely, as stated in the Preamble: 'fairness, social justice' as well as the 'moral foundations of society'.

We now turn to an attempt to explore the normative linkage upon which these two concepts rest. The anti-corruption and human rights approaches share a universal normative framework, but this has yet not been investigated in the contemporary corruption literature (Carmona 2009, p. 330). An early attempt at exploring the normative basis between human rights and anti-corruption was provided by Rajagopal, who connected the two via the concept of state legitimacy, referring to anti-corruption and human rights discourses as two sides of the 'legitimacy coin', arguing both to have the same 'intellectual pedigree' (1999, p. 498).

The substance of this hypothetical coin is what we want to explore, digging to the core norm shared by the two discourses. If we begin with a bird's-eye view of the two discourses, the overarching pattern between the human rights and anti-corruption norms is an inverse relationship. Where there is a prevalence of corruption, there tends to be infringements of human rights. Furthermore, the two discourses are in and of themselves restraints on state power, where human rights discourse is concerned with the violation of *private* rights by public power on the one hand. On the other hand, the anti-corruption discourse focus is on the abuse of *public* office for private gain.

However, an interesting observation gauged from the limited scholarship that has sprung up around this nexus involves some common keywords such as 'discrimination', 'justice' and 'morality'. The morality argument is one that we will not enter upon because it ties the entire discussion to relativistic arguments, where different cultures can have different moralities. What is to our interest are the remaining two – discrimination and justice. These two are intricately linked, and it is the former that could be more easily judged to be applicable to both human rights and corruption.

The expression of the normative basis linking both human rights and anti-corruption is seen most concisely in the legal tools developed. Both human rights and anti-corruption codes focus on the right to non-discrimination and equality before the law, with specific categories of rights and where the right to impartial treatment by public officials is one such category of fundamental rights. In accordance with this, every individual is entitled to be treated according to the principle of equality before the law by public officials. For example, in the case of a person paying a bribe to a public official, this individual then gains a 'privileged status in relation to other similarly placed individuals who have not partaken in bribery' (Gebeye 2012, p. 29). Thus, this is to be considered to be a violation of human rights (in the example, the rights of those individuals who cannot afford to pay such bribes) and as corruption.

The term 'discrimination' as used in the human rights covenants means any distinction or exclusion that has the purpose/effect of impairing/nullifying the recognition/enjoyment by all persons, on an equal footing, of all rights and freedoms.[1] More accurately, '[A]ll individuals possess the right to equality and non-discrimination' (ICCPR, Articles 2.1, 3 and 26, and ICESCR, Article 2.2). Discrimination or, more correctly, the right to remain free from discrimination is explicitly listed by both human rights covenants. The linkage to corruption is, as we see it, direct, where, as Bacio-Terracino (2008) points out, a corrupt act intrinsically carries a distinction, exclusion and/or preference – effectively resulting in discrimination of an individual. Put differently, corruption is about different forms of discrimination, and human rights are about one's right to remain free of discrimination.

Furthermore, the prohibition against discrimination is central to civil, political, economic, social as well as cultural rights. With respect to civil and political rights, it has an independent status because it must not necessarily be related to the enjoyment of a right protected by the ICCPR. Any different treatment that cannot be justified on reasonable grounds will therefore violate the covenant. With respect to economic, social and cultural rights, the prohibition of discrimination is not subject to progressive realization, according to a state's maximum available resources, which means that states infringe the ICESCR whenever discrimination takes place. It is an immediate obligation, which unachieved, per definition results in a human rights violation

---

[1]  See UN Human Rights Committee, General Comment 18, Non-disc. 1989, paragraph 7.

(De Beco 2011, p. 1112). In addition to this, Gebeye (2012, p. 10) presents the implications of corruption as 'discrimination, injustice and disrespect for human dignity', thereby reiterating the normative link that underlies both concepts.

The concept of discrimination ostensibly fares well in linking the two norms. However, upon closer inspection, the intricate link of discrimination (or the lack thereof) is ultimately tied in with the idea of justice. This leads us to one of the more interesting questions that we think has urgent relevance for the choice of policies for anti-corruption movements, namely, how can anti-corruption become an internationally accepted norm in the same manner as human rights have become? This could hopefully result in a political situation where citizens demand a 'corruption-free' society as a matter of their intrinsic rights, where a 'corruption free society' is viewed as a public good. For this to work, it is important that both the scholarly community and various anti-corruption policy organization can (1) recognize the existence of various forms of corruption, (2) understand that while different, these various forms of corruption have a common core related to issues about discrimination and favouritism and (3) make the connection between this 'core of corruption' and the human rights discourse.

# 5 | Corruption as the Connecting Core

In the preceding chapters we elaborated on what we understand to be the 'core' understanding of corruption and its opposite – that is, injustice and justice. Through this understanding, we have been able to link corruption to the human rights discourse as well as the human costs involved as consequence of the spread of corruption. In this chapter we build on this core as the main thrust in our argument of using corruption as an umbrella concept to connect closely related concepts such as clientelism, patronage, state capture and patrimonialism.

As mentioned earlier, a problem for the 'over-definition' of corruption is how to bring together the different forms of corruption, such as clientelism, patronage and patrimonialism, onto one analytical landscape. These concepts all share a core with corruption, which is why they constantly are examined hand-in-hand (Kawata 2006; Kitschelt and Wilkinson 2007; Kotkin and Sajó 2002).

Our main argument is that corruption can serve as a core concept that links together parts of what in other theoretical approaches is defined as forms of illegitimate use of power. When surveying the literature addressing these concepts, we see rough patterns in the application of these concepts geographically. Clientelism seems to be the main form of corruption found in the transition countries of Southeast Asia and Latin America, as well as in post-communist states. Patrimonialism appears to be the form of corruption that dominates the African continent, and patronage is the form of corruption that is found in both developing and developed countries. As Michael Johnston (2005) has argued, we can think of this admittedly huge variation as different 'syndromes of corruption'. However, in relation to developed countries, patronage is a form of legal corruption that appears to go hand-in-hand with 'machine politics' and the mass party. All these concepts stand for different types of corruption that are not explicitly labelled as such. However, they are treated within the literature in the same theoretical space, creating confusion as to what distinguishes them. As Hilgers points out,

A concept should be catchy, intuitively clear and hold to the established characteristics with which it is associated. It should be expressed according to a core characteristic, on which secondary characteristics depend (interdependence) and be easily identifiable with its empirical manifestations. (2011, p. 569)

All these secondary concepts can be argued to be the causes of 'real' or 'true' corruption. They are, however, established concepts in their own right that have a certain degree of overlap with corruption that is not fully explored or explicitly stated within the literature. Therefore, the attempt of the coming chapters is to fill this gap by first delineating the different conceptualizations of these forms of corruption (i.e. clientelism, patronage, patrimonialism, state capture and particularism) as concepts in their own right and describing the core elements of each. This will be followed by an analysis of the evolution of each respective concept parallel to corruption. Finally, we will analyze the overlap that exists between each of them and corruption.

## Corruption and Clientelism

Clientelism, like corruption, has a very negative image. Similar to corruption, clientelism was first viewed as a phenomenon mainly present in developing countries such as in Latin America and Southeast Asia, as well as countries in transition (Landé 1983). Clientelism was developed as a conceptual tool for understanding traditional societies (as is evidenced by the initial anthropological and sociological case studies) where patron-client relationships were observed as social structures. Seen from the lens of modernization theory, it was assumed that it was a phenomenon that would eventually dissipate once a society began to modernize (Hilgers 2011, p. 570). This, however, has not been the case. Instead, as research on the subject has increased, it has become apparent that clientelism is not confined to a certain evolutionary continuum of states' development but is a phenomenon found in both developing and developed countries and at different levels within societies and in various forms. The forms vary from the basic understanding of how political systems work with secondary concepts such as pork-barrelling and special interest politics in a Western country such as the United States (Hopkin 2006, p. 3). As Van de Walle (2000, p. 50) aptly summarized, '[C]lientelism exists in all polities. The form it takes, its extent and its political functions vary enormously, however, across time and place.'

In order to understand how and why clientelism is so closely associated with corruption, it is important to first define what clientelism actually is. According to Hopkin (2006, p. 2), '[P]olitical clientelism describes the distribution of selective benefits to individuals or clearly defined groups in exchange for political support.' Muno (2010, p. 3) defines clientelism as a type of informal institution: '[C]lientelism is a social relationship based on informal rules.' The term has served varied uses – as shorthand for systems, institutions or individuals that are somehow less than ideal (e.g. clientelistic party systems, clientelistic political parties or a clientelistic politician) (Hicken 2011, p. 290; cf. Hydén 2009). The wide and diverse application of the term has resulted not only in confusion and controversy (Hopkins 2006) but also in a blurring of the concept to such an extent that in Hilgers (2011, p. 568) words, '[C]lientelism is no longer clearly differentiated from neighbouring terms, making it a poor concept [that is] difficult to operationalize and to use for theory building.'

Effectively, there is no single agreed-upon definition for what exactly constitutes clientelism (much like corruption). However, there is a set of core elements/characteristics that forms the core concept of clientelism on which these definitions build: dyadic relationships, contingency, hierarchy and iteration.

## The Dyadic Relationships

With its roots in sociological and anthropological studies of traditional societies, the initial focus of clientelism was on the dyadic social relationship between the patron and client at the micro level (Landé 1983). A 'patron' (or 'Big Man') is someone who uses resources (both material and immaterial) that he or she owns or controls and which are available to the client under certain circumstances. These can include assistance, protection, opportunities for career advancement and, of course, money. The client typically gains access to these resources by showing political support – many times in exchange for one's vote or otherwise, such as helping improve the patron's reputation. The emphasis, as Hicken (2011) elaborates, was on the face-to-face interactions between the patron and client, reinforcing a 'personal' and yet 'instrumental friendship' (Scott 1972) between both parties. This dyadic relationship is expanded by many scholars to include brokers, extending clientelism into a triadic relationship.

Weingrod (1968) conceptualized the difference between traditional dyadic relations and modern party-directed clientelism, being one of the first to allude to explicit variables and forms of clientelism. This new model changed the patron-client relationship to that of patron-broker-client relationship (Hydén 2009; Kitschelt and Wilkinson 2007; Muno 2010; Weingrod 1968). In this relationship, the broker acts as the go-between to patron and client, a middleman who arranges exchange of resources between the two parties that may be separated by geographical distance or perhaps in situations where one patron has multiple clients. As Kettering (1988) explains, brokers use resources that they do not directly control themselves. More importantly, brokers play a multifaceted role when playing client to the patron (patron-broker) and patron to the client. The core of this triadic relationship, it is argued, is still the dyadic relationship, where, instead of the direct patron-client relationship, the dyadic relationship between patron-broker and client-broker is paramount (Kettering 1988, p. 426).

The brokerage model evolved in response to the 'levels of analysis problem' that had earlier been one of the main shortcomings identified in the literature (Kaufman 1972). This resulted in a model that could extrapolate the dyadic relationship from the micro to the macro levels of analysis, where the brokerage model is used in analyses of macro scale (with the political party as the patron and the voters as clients), while the dyadic is best suited for the micro-sociological levels. A parallel pattern that can be observed within the literature is the use of the dyadic model for analyses of developing countries, whereas the triadic model is used to analyze the presence of clientelism in more established democracies such as Italy (Caciagli 2006).

## Contingency

The second core aspect shared by most definitions of clientelism is that of reciprocity – that is, the quid pro quo nature (tit for tat) of the relationship (Hicken 2011; Hydén 2009; Kettering 1988; Roniger 2004). The delivery of a good/service by either patron or client is contingent upon the delivery of such from the other, whether in the present or in the future. One of the many descriptions of this reciprocal feature of the relationship is offered by Kaufman:

It is based on the principle of reciprocity; that is, it is a self-regulating form of interpersonal exchange, the maintenance of which depends on the return that each actor expects to obtain by rendering goods and services to the other. (Kaufman 1972, p. 285)

The patron supplies goods/services/jobs in exchange for political support (most often in the form of the client's vote). The politician delivers benefits to the clients that support the politician, and the client supports the politician that delivers on his or her promises. In the clientelistic relationship, there are always strings attached.

The type of good or service exchanged can vary from material (ranging from cash to something as random as cutlery) to non-material benefits such as protection, education, healthcare or admission to a school (Muno 2010). The exchange, however, does not have to occur simultaneously; there can be a time lag where the exchange may be completed in the near future. A client may have voted in favour of his or her patron upon the promise of receiving certain benefits once the patron is voted into office. This results in two imperative aspects of the clientelistic relationship. Firstly, there is the need for each party to monitor and sanction the other, as well as an implicit trust between the two, which is strengthened by the on-going nature of the relationship (iteration).

## Iteration

Iteration is the one aspect that sets clientelism apart from other exchange relationships that involve corruption. The relationship between the client and patron is an on-going one. This is shown by the fact that the exchange does not have to take place simultaneously. This 'future' aspect has important implications. It creates a situation in which the future is considered in the relationship, which is different from a one-time payment of a bribe. Effectively, each party has the opportunity to establish its reliability. This repeated interaction not only reinforces social norms of reciprocity but also results in an element of trust between both parties. Furthermore, the iteration aspect provides opportunities for predictability and monitoring for both parties (Eisenstadt and Roniger 1984, pp. 48–9). After an election, a client can monitor whether the patron fulfilled his or her election promises (upon which the client had voted for the politician/patron). If the politician has delivered on the promise, then the client will vote for the politician again. The same goes for patrons, but due to the nature of voting, if the ballot is secret, the politicians will only be able to tell whether specific local groups of voters kept their promise to vote for them or not. In the same way, '[R]epeated interactions over time allow politicians to observe which voters keep their promises and which voters can be swayed, and calibrate the size of offer needed to sway the voters' (Hicken 2011, p. 293).

## Hierarchy

Hierarchy has been a central feature in defining clientelism. Roniger (2004, p. 353), for example, defines 'clientelism' as 'involve[ing] asymmetric but mutually beneficial relationships of power and exchange, a non-universalistic quid pro quo between individuals or groups of unequal standing'. Caciagli (2006) further elaborates the asymmetry of the relationship between patron and client, defining 'clientelism' as informal power relations between individuals or groups in unequal positions based on exchange of benefits (cf. Kawata 2006, p. 157). Somebody with higher status (the patron) takes advantage of his or her authority and resources to protect and benefit somebody with an inferior status (the client), who reciprocates with support and services. The relationship can be both voluntary and coercive and based upon particular interests, such as a common ethnicity (Habyarimana et al. 2009). This asymmetry is reinforced by the patron-client relationship being described as 'exploitative' and one of 'domination', as well as diction that emphasises 'obligation' and 'loyalty' when describing the role of the client (Kitschelt 2000; Stokes 2007). Other scholars, such as Kettering, are more direct, describing the asymmetry as 'a patron is the superior and a client the inferior in an unequal, vertical, and reciprocal relationship' (Kettering 1988, p. 425).

Recently, the focus of research has shifted from hierarchy itself to that of the shifting nature of hierarchy, or what some scholars label 'old clientelism' versus 'new clientelism' (Hopkin 2006; Kawata 2006). This refers to the shift in power from a vertical dyadic relationship to one that is horizontal, with the client in a much stronger position than before. A fitting case is that of Italy – where clients with higher incomes and living standards, effectively no longer tied by the burden of 'loyalty', are able to shop for patrons, weighing what politician offers better stakes. As a result, Piatonni (2001) argues, patrons are now in a weaker position where clients choose to enter the clientelistic deal in order to get privileged access to public resources. This is what Hopkin (2006) refers to as 'vote for exchange'.

Scholars such as Kitschelt and Wilkinson (2007) change the power dynamic when analyzing clientelism through the lens of principal-agent, where the client effectively is the principal and the patron the agent, clients holding power over politicians through their vote. This model could be useful in situations such as the case in Italy, where voters use their votes to shop for patrons who can offer them a better deal. However, in situations where the relationship is not voluntary and the relationship is entered upon as a coping mechanism by the client who needs access to public resources as basic as water and electricity (e.g. a villager in a developing country dependent upon the local landlord), then this principal-agent model may be troublesome. In the latter situation, the client is in the weaker position, and asymmetry is blatantly apparent.

However, Muno (2010, p. 5) found the principal-agent model to be a suitable tool for the patron-client relationship when applied to the brokerage system, 'with the patron as the principal instructing the broker as the agent with the management of his affairs'. In these clientelistic pyramids (aka 'brokerage systems'), the hierarchal relationship is retained, with the patrons situated at the top and the brokers/agents in the middle with clients at the bottom.

Corruption and clientelism are different notions. Clientelism is a form of social organization, whereas corruption is an individual social behaviour (where you are your own client, trying to play patron to yourself) that may or may not grow into a mass phenomenon. One can imagine clientelism without corruption, although the two often go hand-in-hand. In the post-communist context, the two phenomena seem fused at the hip (Sajó 2003, p. 2) Clientelism and corruption are two separate concepts that have an overlap, evidenced by the constant comparison/connection of them, as shown by the abundance of research focused on comparing the two concepts (Della Porta and Vannucci 1999; Kawata 2006; Kotkin and Sajó 2002; Singer 2009). It is within the space of this overlap that they are confused. The overlap has different degrees, and some scholars define clientelism as a structural form of corruption (Karklins 2005; Sajó 2004) where the overlap makes separation of the two concepts difficult (Sajó 2003). A lighter degree of overlap focuses on the general comparison between the two, where the focus lies on the similarities of the concepts in their own right as well as the overlap they share. Finally, others have tried to verify the link by exploring empirical similarities (Singer 2009).

The most difficult overlap between corruption and clientelism to explore is that where clientelism is a type of corruption. This conceptual space is the prevalent one applied in the research to the studies of post-communist states, where clientelism is described as a structural form of corruption (Mungiu-Pippidi 2006, 2011). Here the concepts are dependent upon each other, with clientelism as a form of social organization and corruption seen as a form of individual social behaviour. As a structural feature of a society, it focuses on the social aspect of corruption. This dependency is further highlighted by the catch-22 model presented by Della Porta and Vannuci (1999), that is, clientelism → increase of exchange votes → increases in the cost of politics → (supply of corruption) → availability of money for politicians' → incentives to buy votes → clientelism (cf. Kawata 2006, p. 13). The model points to clientelism as conducive to corruption.

As pointed out by Hicken, clientelism can drive corruption via three different paths. Firstly, certain clientelistic exchanges can be outright illegal, such as vote buying. Secondly, by 'undermining the ability of citizens to hold public officials accountable', Hicken further argues that clientelism may in fact be creating 'a culture of impunity' within which it is harder to punish individuals for corrupt behaviour. Thirdly, as is demonstrated in the aforementioned model, the demand for resources (needed to facilitate an exchange between client and patron) could work as a driver for politicians to use corrupt ways to acquire more resources. A suitable example that demonstrates the overlap between clientelism and corruption is the Chinese practice of *guanxi*.

This ancient term refers to the informal institution of personal networks in which a system of exchange exists around mutual services and the acceptance of a debt obligation. These networks are normally based on personal relations stemming from factors such as common village or region, having gone to the same school, being in the same association or having served in the same military unit (somewhat reminiscent of the fraternity culture prevalent in many developed countries such as the United States). It is said to be deeply rooted in the Chinese culture, strongly tied in with the concept of honour/'losing face', where the debt obligation is ensured through one's social reputation, superimposed on the will to maintain 'face' in the group and with peers. If one were to obtain a favour through their *guanxi* network and choose not to repay this debt, one would not only lose face but also would risk losing access to the network as a whole, which tends to be part of one's social networking as well. It is this informal institution that has been the focus of much of the corruption studies centred on China, where *guanxi* is understood to be conducive to corruption. Because *guanxi* networks share many clientelistic characteristics, it is tempting to label *guanxi* as the Chinese form of clientelism ('brokerage model'). However, an aspect that is debated within the literature is the essential characteristic of hierarchy in a clientelistic relationship that is absent in the case of *guanxi* – the favour/service can be obtained from anyone. Pye (1981) argues that *guanxi* does not have a clear-cut vertical relationship between the members of the network, explaining that the hierarchy can be very subtle. However, Landé (1983, 441) does not consider the vertical/horizontal to be such a decisive factor for the relationship to be clientelistic:

In my opinion there is no clear break between vertical and horizontal dyads, and their structural and behavioural similarities are more important than their differences. I use the term 'horizontal dyadic alliances' simply because the conventional term 'patron-client relationship' connotes a vertical tie. Others may take a different view. (Landé 1983, p. 441)

The strong overlap that presents itself, where clientelism is considered conducive to corruption, is empirically tested by Singer (2009, p. 14), who finds this link to be very weak (or even non-existent): '[W]e find no evidence that clientelism may potentially create an atmosphere conducive to corruption via its effect on the rule of law or political accountability.' Thus, there can be a high degree of clientelism without corruption but probably not high degrees of corruption without clientelism.

Turning to the lower degrees of corruption, scholars have focused their attention on the similarities between the two concepts in order to explain the overlap between them. First of all, both clientelism and corruption concern the crossover between the private and public realms. If corruption is defined as the abuse of public office for private gain, then clientelism stems from the same root: 'its intention to generate "private" revenue for patrons and clients and, as a result, obstruct "public" revenue for members of the general community, who are not a part of the patron-client arrangement' (Kawata 2006, p. 4). This overlap is explained differently by different scholars, one of which focuses on the similarities between the two concepts. One of the main similarities is that the theories followed the same development path. At the outset, both carried negative connotations – anthropologists focusing on clientelism, with political scientists focusing on corruption. Both concepts were viewed as part and parcel of the development stages that states went through, effectively as phenomena that would dissipate once a certain development stage was reached. Contrary to theory, both phenomena persisted despite economic development stages reached, resulting in them once again carrying the negative connotations (Kawata 2006).

Kobayashi (2006) presented a list of similarities between the two. Both exist universally (can be found at the international level as well as local levels) and can be divided into the same typologies; both merge when measuring the scale of political corruption (clientelism is found at the realms of grand corruption); the quantity and form of both change based on time and region; and these changes are due to both cultural effect and socio-political systems. The cultural effects are the issue that needs to be focused upon. Another similarity is found in the fact that measures of corruption are often used as proxies for the extent of clientelism (Keefer 2007).

Other scholars have focused on differentiating the two concepts. One example is offered by Muno, who compared corruption and clientelism with the example of a bribe being exchanged (Muno 2010, pp. 7–8). The lack of personal element and the lack of continuity are elements of corruption that distinguish it from clientelism. In cases of corruption, you do not have to know the 'partner' because he or she can be an unknown police officer who receives a bribe from a car driver/ citizen in order to forge a ticket. The car driver/citizen and police officer may never meet again, whereas patron and client are tight knit, and the process is an iterative one.

Apart from the clientelistic/corruption overlap, there is a further overlap that clientelism shares with patronage, where 'patronage' and 'clientelism' as terms are used interchangeably in the literature (Hilgers 2011). The strongest degree found here is where patronage is identified as a type of clientelistic exchange. Chapter 6 will first venture to define patronage, followed by an exploration of the similarities of corruption and patronage, finally ending with a brief exploration of the similarities between clientelism and patronage.

# 6 | Corruption and Patronage

A second concept with which corruption is often entangled is that of patronage. Patronage means different things in different disciplines. For the anthropologist it is a social relationship (Weingrod 1968), whereas for the political scientist it is a way of governing, an 'electoral tool' or an 'instrument for managing political relations'. Other descriptions are 'organisational or governmental resource' or simply 'the ways in which party politicians distribute public jobs or special favours in exchange for electoral support' (Arriola 2009; Hydén 2009; Kopecky and Scherlis 2008; Weingrod 1968, p. 379). For the purposes of this chapter, the political science understanding of patronage is the one that will be used, as it appears to be the one more suitable to contemporary usage. In political science, 'patronage' is a particularistic exchange that takes place between patron and client, where the object of exchange is that of public office; that is, the patron offers public office to the client in exchange for electoral support/political allegiance/etc. It is more simply understood as appointments to positions in the state (Kopecky and Scherlis 2008, p. 356). That which varies is the end for which patronage is exercised. The diversity of ends most often sought are neatly summarized by Souraf:

The chief functions of patronage are: maintaining an active party organization ... Promoting intra-party cohesion ... Attracting voters and supporters ... Financing the party and its candidates ... Procuring favourable government action ... Creating party discipline in policy making. (Souraf 1961, pp. 309–10)

In the literature, patronage is portrayed as a phenomenon closely interlinked with the development stages of a state. Initially patronage, as a subject matter, was characterized as a phenomenon pertaining to developing states. However, a closer look at patronage reveals the phenomenon to be present in almost all polities (Van de Walle 2000) whether developing or not. The scale and form are what varies, the difference stemming from the purpose for which patronage is used, as well as by who plays the role of patron. Therefore, this chapter elaborates on the different ends for which patronage is used: maximization of votes as a means to achieve a stable political landscape, and finally, as a means to strengthen a political party organization.

## Patronage as an Electoral Tool

It can be argued that the practice of patronage as an electoral tool (public office in exchange for votes) has remained the overarching goal of the patronage exercise. In the literature, patronage as an electoral tool is ostensibly a matter of the developmental stages of the state, where the following relationship is applicable (from Golden 2000):

Party/politician → electoral support → material benefit/

office/position in state via state institution

This is the most basic form of patronage, most often attributed to developing states. The setting tends to be rural, where the relationship is centred on the individual patron (landlord/politician) and villagers (citizens), most aptly exemplified by the 'vote banks' that form in developing countries. In these vote banks, the patron gains a strong following as an individual – so strong in fact that if the politician were to change political party, the vote bank would 'travel' with the patron. Excellent examples of this are provided by the vote banks formed in the subcontinent (Weingrod 1968, p. 380).

However, as Weingrod makes clear, the changing characteristic of the patron go hand-in-hand with the developmental stages of the state, resulting in different applications of patronage – in the case from 'traditional' to 'mass' society, where the new patron at this point is the political party and its clientele constitute the 'constituents' (voters). The exercise of patronage by the political party as an electoral tool in modern settings can be exemplified by the patronage exercised by political parties in the United States, more popularly known as 'party machines' – where the relationship is shared between a party (or politician) and its party members or group of potential voters, that is, linkage politics between the party and society (Johnston 1979; Scott 1972). A further example of patronage in modern settings (i.e. developed states) is the case study of Italy, where 'political patronage ... is typically offered exclusively to known or potential party loyalists, and it explicitly functions as one side of an exchange of public resources for votes' (Golden 2000, p. 11; cf. Golden 2003).

## Patronage as a Stabilizing Tool

A different approach to patronage is to use it as a stabilizing tool. According to Arriola (2009, p. 1340), '[T]he use of patronage as an instrument for managing political relations needs to be explained', reasoning that 'relatively little is known about the extent to which the distribution of patronage systematically affects political stability.' Arriola's research centred upon the African continent, in which context the use of patronage as a stabilization tool is found very much within the developing countries, where the hierarchy of citizen → political elite → top leader (aka 'big man') is very much intact. The literature has remained divided on the use of patronage as a stabilizing tool, one school perceiving patronage as a source of instability due to its 'distortion of economic policies and political institutions' (Arriola 2009, p. 1344) and another, at the other end of the spectrum, viewing it as a stabilizing tool, arguing: 'the distribution of patronage could be used to pull together a heterogeneous elite and in this way build up institutions over the long term' (Arriola 2009, p. 1344). Arriola investigates patronage as a tool for achieving stability within the political elite by using state resources to 'facilitate intra-elite accommodation' to reign in the political instability that occurs from 'elite disagreement over the distribution of power and resources' (Arriola 2009, p. 1341). The importance of the political elites' satisfaction is centred upon the 'gap' they fill in the political structure – typically as intermediaries between the rulers and the public – as part of a 'patronage pyramid':

Power is . . . arrayed through a system of relations linking rulers not with the 'public' or even with the ruled (at least not directly), but with patrons, associates, clients, supporters, and rivals, who constitute the 'system'. (Jackson and Rosberg 1982, p. 19)

The purpose of intra-elite accommodation is twofold. Firstly, it decreases the risk of being ousted from office via extra-constitutional means. Secondly it ensures less dependency on the loyalty of specific members of the political elite, effectively spreading out the risk/eggs into many different baskets. Although Arriola (2009) focuses on the

African continent, he points out that this model is useful in the context of non-African states as well – whether this be Asia, Latin America or the Middle East.

## Patronage as Organizational Resource Tool

The form of patronage, most related and researched within the context of developed states, is that of patronage as a resource tool for government. Here the political party plays the role of patron that uses patronage towards achieving various aims.

One of the earlier studies focusing on this is that of Weingrod (1968). He compared and contrasted how patronage as a tool for governing is used in the so-called traditional sense (between patron-client) juxtaposed against the modern setting of party patronage. The focus is on the evolution of patronage in relation to the transition from traditional to modern settings, in this case the change in patron, where the party now exercises patronage instead of a single person per se. Within more primitive settings, patronage can be used as a political tool for centralizing a state or applicable to state structures – so-called cellular structures, such as federalist or decentralized ones (where the multiple layers effectively have 'gaps' acting as the 'space' for patronage to emerge). The mediating function serves a practical purpose in settings where the physical infrastructure of the state may not be well established – for example, a primitive transportation system. Weingrod provides a succinct description of the different types of states that foster different kinds of patronage:

[T]raditional patron-client ties can be seen to arise within a state structure in which authority is dispersed and state activity limited in scope, and in which considerable separation exists between the levels of village, city and state. Party-directed patronage, on the other hand, is associated with the expanding scope and general proliferation of state activities, and also with the growing integration of village, city and state. (1968, p. 381)

In effect, the more segmented a state structure is, the more 'gaps' exist, resulting in the creation of spaces for patronage to arise, where patronage helps to integrate the state. The patron not only plays the role of mediator between the village level and the state apparatus but actually is contributing to the integration of the different levels of the state, whether between village and town or town and city – 'cohesive-fying' the state.

The use of patronage as a tool of governing is not merely limited to governing and organizing a state because it can be used at various organizational levels, for example, in political parties or trade unions. In this capacity it acts as an organizational tool to strengthen the patronage organization itself. This is exemplified by the early European example of Sardinia:

[T]he Party's monopoly of thousands of jobs, and the special privileges given to loyal Fascists in securing posts and winning promotions, meant that the party had become the major dispenser of political patronage, through which the party also became an increasingly coordinated structure. (Weingrod 1968, p. 393)

The access to thousands of state jobs and public resources not only strengthens the political party but effectively also leverages the political party into a position where it can use these resources to 'serve [its] own electoral ends' (Weingrod 1968, p. 384) Another fitting example is that of political machines in the United States, which use patronage as a means to strengthen the party's position by using public jobs as both organizational maintenance and an electoral tool (Johnston 1979). A similar trend had developed in Spain, where the conflict about the control of such patronage jobs seems to have been a major factor behind the outbreak of the Spanish Civil War in 1936 (Lapuente and Rothstein 2014).

Some of the more recent research carried out by Kopecky et al. (2012) investigates the use of patronage as an organizational resource. This angle focuses on patronage in the modern context, as a mode of governing where the political party serves as patron, but contrary to linkage politics between party and society, the focus is on party-state linkages. In this case, patronage 'represents a form of institutional control or of institutional exploitation that operates to the benefit of the party organisation' (Kopecký et al. 2012, p. 7). Patronage thus is 'a strategy to build parties' organisational networks in the public and semi-public sphere' in order to ultimately control the policies that the state churns out:

[P]atronage is for contemporary parties a mode of governing, a process by which the party acquires a voice in, and gains feedback from, the various policy-making forums that characterise the modern multilevel governance systems. (Kopecký et al. 2012, p. 11)

This is the predominant form of patronage found in European and other modern political settings, where social and political conditions are not dire enough to use patronage as an electoral tool, that is, as an electoral resource to collect/maximize votes. Instead, the ultimate interest is to have control over the policymaking process. The 'permeation' of the aforementioned patronage (in this case, the reach of political parties into the state through the allocation of jobs in both the public and semipublic sectors) varies greatly within Europe (Kopecky and Scherlis 2008). In the Scandinavian countries, the reach of patronage is limited to small number of positions in the top echelons, whereas the former communist states such as Hungary and Latvia present cases where there is deep permeation of party patronage within the state. By ensuring political control of the policy implementation process, patronage is used as a mode of governing. In the former example only the top echelons of state positions are patronage based, whereas the latter cases entail an almost complete change of much of the public positions within the bureaucracy, resulting in a thoroughly politicized civil service.

The preceding application of patronage is by no means comprehensive, but it points in the direction of the multifaceted ends to which patronage is applied. As our interest is to investigate how patronage overlaps with the concept of corruption, the aforementioned manifold usages of patronage should alleviate how and in what ways certain forms of patronage can be considered corrupt and for what reasons, helping to narrow down in a precise manner where the overlap between the two concepts occurs.

A good starting point for exploring the overlap between patronage and corruption – patronage and clientelism – is the following quotation from Médard, which incorporates the different forms of corruption: 'Corruption takes many forms; clientelism, nepotism, ethnic and other favouritism are all variants of corruption, in social terms' (Médard 1998, p. 308).

## Patronage and Corruption

[P]atronage and corruption may in practice closely follow one another, as for example when patronage appointments are made for the purpose of providing private kickbacks or in return for bribes. In a similar vein, patronage is an important supporting condition for the survival of systemic corruption, in that it is through the appointment of bureaucrats and other state personnel loyal to party politicians that operations designed to pace checks on the activities of politicians are often effectively covered up.

– Kopecký et al. (2012, p. 9)

Patronage and corruption overlap, but this overlap is of different types. Patronage can at times 'lead' to corruption, while at other times it in itself is corruption. As a starting point, the concept of party patronage is not as penetrating as corruption because it is done in the open and not under the table, as most corruption deals are. However, the overlap into corruption is obvious when these appointments are done 'for the purpose of providing private kickbacks' or more so 'in return for bribes'. Furthermore, as Kopecky and Scherlis point out, '[P]atronage is the necessary condition for the emergence of the three particularistic exchanges [clientelism, pork barrel and corruption] since it is mainly due to their ability to control state positions that parties are able to manipulate state resources in clientelistic or corrupt ways' (Kopecky and Scherlis 2008, p. 357). A situation where patronage is within its legal limits but leaning more strongly towards being corruption is provided by Golden (2000, p. 17):

Italy's post-war patronage system probably functioned more on the margin of legality than completely beyond it. The outcome was nonetheless that by the 1980s, the bulk of appointments to the public sector were taking place in clear violation of the spirit of civil service regulations even if in nominal conformity to legal requirements.

This effectively becomes the root to the survival of systemic corruption in these systems. Table 6.1 neatly summarizes the concepts highlighting how patronage differs from corruption and where it overlaps, providing an easy overview of the concepts and how they are interrelated.

## Patronage and Clientelism

Our effort so far has been to specify how corruption relates parallel concepts and we must briefly elaborate on one of the clearest overlaps we have found. This is between patronage and clientelism, a connection that many scholars tend to overlook but we want to highlight. However, the

Table 6.1 *Overview of Different Concepts Related to Patronage*

|  | Patronage | Clientelism | Corruption |
|---|---|---|---|
| State resource | Jobs in state institutions | Subsidies, loans, medicines, food, public-sector jobs | Public decisions |
| Goal of patron | Control of institutions, reward of (organizational) loyalty | Electoral support | Financial resources |
| Recipients (clients) | Anybody | Party voters | Companies, entrepreneurs |
| Legal status | Legal or illegal | Legal or illegal | Illegal |
| Currency of exchange | Work | Vote | Bribe |

*Source:* Adapted from Kopecký et al. (2012).

point to be reiterated is that these two, although similar, are independent concepts in their own right. This difference in understanding is pointed out as an imperative aspect that must be taken into account when analyzing patronage because 'the perspectives of the two disciplines are ... exceedingly different ones. It is therefore important to be clear about these distinctions and explore their implications' (Weingrod 1968, p. 378). Such a treatment will not be carried out here, but it should be pointed out that this comparative approach helps to alleviate *why* the term 'patronage' is so closely associated to the concept of clientelism. Not only are the terms 'clientelism' and 'patronage' used interchangeably, but at times some scholars specify patronage as a type of clientelistic exchange in which a client's vote is given in exchange for public office. This close relationship, or indeed overlap of concepts, can be traced to the anthropological understanding of patronage as elaborated by Weingrod:

[T]he study of patronage as phrased by anthropologists is the analysis of how persons of unequal authority, yet linked through ties of interest and friendship, manipulate their relationships in order to attain their ends. (Weingrod 1968, p. 378)

In the literature, patronage is most often interchangeably used with clientelism. The statement that the two are coterminous relates to the fact that the distribution of state jobs had in some cases in the past been used on a mass scale for electoral purposes (e.g. post-war Italy or the era of American city machines) (Kopecký et al. 2012, p. 9).

# 7 | *Corruption and Patrimonialism*

The term 'patrimonialism' was brought back into political science and sociology by Roth in his attempt to 'examine an older term for [its] contemporary usefulness' (Roth 1968, p. 194). It is a term for one of Max Weber's typologies for traditional authority/governing modes or, as Roth puts it, 'the actual operating modes and administrative arrangements by which rulers 'govern' (Roth 1968, p. 156). Max Weber defined 'patrimonialism' as

a special case of patriarchal domination – domestic authority decentralised through assignment of land and sometimes of equipment to sons of the house or other dependents. (Weber 1922/1978, p. 1011)

Weber's original definition extrapolated patriarchal domination onto a larger canvas, effectively from the scale of the household to investigate social structures and systems for governing (state level), where the model was applied to the heterogeneous empires, such as the Roman and Ottoman, in order to analyze the systems for governing.

Patrimonialism is a concept that is constantly used as a synonym for, as well as interchangeably with, corruption, especially in the context of explaining the embeddedness of corruption in the African continent. In fact, some scholars refer to patrimonialism as a 'theory of corruption' that can 'explain corruption in relation to the supposed specificity of African political systems' (Bracking 2007). However, using such a narrow approach not only does injustice to the concept but also negates the fact that, like clientelism and patronage, patrimonialism too is a concept in its own right.

Over the years, the concept has undergone various applications as well as different ways of nuancing. Some scholars have applied it as a universal concept applicable to all countries, whether developing or developed (Erdman and Engel 2007; Pitcher 2009; Roth 1968). In an early seminal study of Nigeria, Joseph (1987) uses the term 'prebendalism' to describe the same phenomenon. Others have used patrimonialism as a particularistic concept limited to developing countries (Roth 1968; Theobald 1982), and some have treated it as a region-specific concept, specifically as an African phenomenon (Bratton and Van de Walle 1994; Erdman and Engel 2007).

The essence of patrimonialism that pervades the scholarship and unites the previously described applications and nuances is succinctly summarized by Theobald (1982, p. 552):

The essential feature of patrimonial regimes [is] ... the exchange of resources (jobs, promotions, titles, contracts, licenses, immunity from the law, etc.) between key figures in government and strategically located individuals: trade union leaders, businessmen, community leaders, and so forth. In return for these resources, the government or heads of state receive economic and political support. The emphasis is on the personal nature of the exchange: virtually all the analyses that have resorted to the term have been informed, either explicitly or implicitly, by the model of the patron-client relationship.

As this quotation clarifies, the concept of patrimonialism is based on the basic patron-client model. It can be viewed as a metamorphosis of clientelism and patronage or perhaps as encompassing these character-istics of the two concepts. The difference, however, lies within *who* is exercising it. Since patrimonialism is a mode of governing derived from the concept of patriarchy, the focus is upon the 'head' of the organiza-tion. Like Aristotle, Weber too viewed governing in opposites and took it a step further when investigating the grey zones that perpetuate within society – in this case within the theory of patrimonialism. Scholars today have continued to use this comparative outlook by juxtaposing patrimonial and rational-legal structures in most of the research surrounding the concept. Table 7.1 neatly summarizes the differences between patrimonialism and the rational-legal models.

That which differs between the various scholars over and above the aforementioned applications is the difference of degrees pertaining to the focus on the more personalistic character of patrimonialism (North et al. 2009; Roth 1968), whereas some encouraged an inclusion of a broader perspective by including socio-economic features of states (Theobald 1982). It should be noted that Table 7.1 is limited to explor-ing the administrative aspect of states, whereas the scholarship sur-rounding patrimonialism tends to focus on the governing system as a whole.

**Table 7.1** *The Patrimonial and Bureaucratic Models of Administration*

| Patrimonial | Rational-legal bureaucratic |
|---|---|
| • Administrators are recruited and promoted as reward for personal connections with political leaders. | • Administrators are recruited and promoted in competitive processes that judge their merit and expertise. |
| • Administrators can be dismissed for no reason. | • Administrators can only be dismissed with cause. |
| • There is an unspoken hierarchy with little specialization or specification of output and uncertain reporting channels. | • There is an authorized hierarchy with clear division of labour, specific standards for output and well-defined reporting channels. |
| • Important orders may be given orally. | • Important orders are put in writing. |
| • The public and private realms are blurred. | • The public and private realms are kept separate. |
| • Administrators supplement their salaries with bribes and kickbacks. | • Administrators are prohibited from supplementing their salaries. |
| • System is decentralized, allowing wide discretion on the job. | • System is centralized, with little room for discretion on the job. |
| • Administrators' actions are arbitrary, based on subjective reasoning, and follow ad-hoc procedures. | • Administrators' actions are predictable, based on objective methods, and follow uniform procedures. |
| • Rules are applied with partiality, and some citizens get preferential treatment. | • Rules are applied with neutrality, and all citizens receive equal treatment. |
| • Verbal agreements are used in government procurement and sales. | • Binding legal contracts are used in government procurement and sales. |

*Source:* Adapted from Brinkerhoff and Goldsmith (2002).

## Degrees of Separation?

The nuances that differentiate the scholars, apart from the aforementioned applications, lie within the different degrees of patrimonial and rational-legal aspects (whether a system is 50–50, 30–70, etc.) that exist as the structural framework for each case investigated. If one were to put these different patrimonial systems on a scale, the differentiation would be a matter of degrees. On one end of the spectrum there is the traditionalist patrimonialism or 'pure patrimonialism', wherein the rational-legal structure is almost entirely absent. As Roth (1968, p. 196) pointed out, '[I]n terms of traditional political theory [such states] may be private governments of those powerful enough to rule.' These are differentiated from the rational-legal bureaucracies 'in that neither constitutionally regulated legislation nor advancement on the basis of training and efficiency need be predominant in public administration'. As for the 'corruption scale', this would be a state that is considered very corrupt, where the bureaucracy of the state is organized not by meritocracy but by politicization. This is the type that is most prevalent in developing countries (or, as Roth points out, 'new states') that is mostly associated with corruption. As per Roth (1968, p. 197) himself: 'Such personal governance easily evokes notions of opportunism and corruption from the perspective of charismatic or legal-rational legitimation.'

On the other end of the spectrum is Erdmann and Engel's (2007) model, introducing modern-day patrimonialism, which they term 'neo-patrimonialism'. This new term is used for multiple reasons, the first of which is to differentiate it from Weber's original typology of patrimonialism and to highlight that the neo-patrimonialism to which they refer is the contemporary form of patrimonialism. Unlike Weber's 'pure' ideal types, neo-patrimonialism constitutes a hybrid – a system in which there is a fully established structure of the ideal type legal-rational bureaucracy, but the governing mode itself has patrimonial features. In other words, there is in place an established system, a so-called rational-legal structure, but most of the decision-making processes (in issues such as the selection of civil servants, decisions about public policies and their implementation) are exercised with a patrimonial flavour. This model creates uncertainty and a lack of predictability as the external appearance is one of the ideal, impartial rational-legal, whereas in practice, power within the system is exercised according to the personal preferences of the leader instead of following the prescribed laws in place.

## The Overlap between Patrimonialism and Corruption

The most complicated overlap within the literature is that of patrimonialism and corruption. The ostensible complication is the apparent similarities that explain the use of the terms as synonyms: both concepts came to the fore during the 1960s and 1970s as issues of the 'other', wherein they were applied to developing states or 'new states'.

From a conceptual approach, the problem is that scholars have assigned patrimonialism as a theory of corruption without systematically comparing the two. The treatment remains limited to a brief sentence or two where the reader is left to decide how or in what manner the patrimonial feature is corrupt. Within contemporary research, the undercurrent that appears to be the reason for patrimonialism to be used synonymously with corruption is that it is a mode of government that conflicts with the ideal type exercised by liberal democratic rule-of-law states. Instead of following Weber's legal-rational model, states that follow the traditional mode of authority (i.e. patrimonialism) are viewed from an evolutionist aspect, where all ills within these states, whether African or not, stem from the root cause of patrimonialism (Pitcher et al. 2009). The ostensible understanding that is deduced is that the patrimonial form of government itself is viewed as a matter of the 'other', wherein the mode of governing itself is seen as corrupt, even if the original reading as propounded by Weber confirms this to be a legitimate form of authority. Instead of acknowledging this by looking beyond the dichotomy presented by Weber, most scholars assert this mode of authority to be corrupt in and of itself, with the way the term has been constantly used alongside corruption, without actually providing evidence to support this claim.

Furthermore, many social scientists add the modifier 'neo' to 'patrimonialism' to distinguish what they regard as a modern variant of Weber's ideal type – one in which a veneer of rational-legal authority has been imposed by colonialism, yet a personalistic or 'patrimonial' logic characterized by patronage, clientelism and corruption is said to prevail – just as it is assumed to have done in the past (Pitcher et al. 2009).

Under a veneer of rational-legal authority imposed by colonialism, a pervasive 'patrimonial' or personalistic logic is said to prevail, encouraging patronage, clientelism, corruption and economic stagnation. Even with the transition to democracy, forms of patrimonialism are still seen as brakes on Africa's future political and economic development (Pitcher et al. 2009, p. 150).

# 8 | Corruption, State Capture and Political Particularism

Of all the preceding side-lying concepts, state capture is the youngest and is viewed as a clear type of corruption, wherein the initial definition offered was as follows: 'shaping the formation of the basic rules of the game (i.e. laws, rules, decrees and regulations) through illicit and non-transparent private payments to public officials' (Hellman 2000). It is the only area that fully encapsulates one of the largest 'grey zones' within corruption research – that is, the interaction of the private and public sectors – a predatory group of individuals (whether in the shape of firms or local elites) and the state itself. The state is captured via policy mechanisms being dictated by, and in favour of, private actors (i.e. firms, local elites) at a significant social cost (cf. Hydén 2009). This results in the private sphere dictating the public sphere. An example of this is lobbying by different interests, which is considered a fundamental part of democracy. However, what remains contested is where the line is drawn, demarcating where it stops being a healthy democratic process versus being seen as corruption. A much-contested example is that of private-sector lobbying in the United States.

The term 'state capture' was coined by researchers at the World Bank (Hellman 2000; Hellman et al. 2000) and brought about in an attempt to investigate the effect of the private sector upon the state. It was specifically within the transition states of the former USSR at the recognition that 'powerful firms have been able to capture the state and collude with public officials to extract rents through the manipulation of state power' (Hellman et al. 2000, p. 1). Another strand of state capture research takes the conceptualization of Hellman et al. (2000) from focusing on economic agents to focusing on agents within a state (cf. Grzymala-Brusse 2008).

Unlike the other side-lying concepts listed previously, that is, other types of corruption that focus on the output side, such as how power is exercised, state capture focuses directly on the *input* side of the equation, where corruption is affecting 'the basic rules of the game (i.e. laws, rules, decrees and regulations)', and public polices from the stage of formation. This difference is essential because it can shift the type of corruption from the illegal sphere to that of being legal, even though in practice it might be considered corrupt by the stakeholders involved. The literature elaborates that the preceding definition is not limited to only firms but is applicable to individuals as well as groups in both private and public sectors in order to influence laws, regulations and other government policies to their own advantage as a result of the 'illicit' and 'non-transparent' provision of private benefits (whether this be money, goods, political advantage, etc.) to public officials (Hellman et al. 2000).

One criticism of this fledgling definition is concerned with payments to public officials where it is a prevalent economic focus, the 'exchange of private payments to public officials'. This empirical focus, as carried out by Hellman et al. (2000) in 'Seize the State, Seize the Day' is based on firm-level data collected through the Business Environment and Enterprise Performance Survey in 1999 in order to understand the relationship between private and public sectors in transitional societies, similar to the majority of literature on the topic. The heavy initial empirical focus left agape a theoretical space as to the normative aspects of the concept.

Furthermore, such a narrow focus leaves out other aspects of state capture, such as that of the local/national/religious elites or economies of religion or a focus that takes into account state capture by religious elites wherein the public's vote is exchanged for salvation in the afterlife, a phenomenon prevalent in Latin America, Africa and much of Asia. One study that has helped to expand the research towards a non-economic focus is that carried out by Grzymala-Brusse (2008), in which the focus has been shifted from economic agents to agents within a state.

## State Capture and Corruption

State capture as a form of corruption can be more harmful than the sources listed earlier because it 'goes beyond excluding the citizens outside the corrupt bargain from a certain political procedure and instead excludes all citizens outside of the group from almost all parts of the political process in general' (Stine 2011). State capture is thus a phenomenon that takes place through the exercise of clientelism or patronage, where a relationship is built up between parties. This understanding may be criticized as narrow because it is activated only through the mechanisms of 'clientelism or patronage'. Therefore, to gain a more thorough insight into this overlap, it can help to zoom out and see state capture/corruption overlap as 'ways in which systems of incentives, or economies of influence, might advance or deter a collective objective' (Lessig 2013, p. 2). Lessig goes on to label the input side of corruption as 'institutional corruption', defining it as

a systemic and strategic influence which is legal, or even currently ethical, that undermines the institution's effectiveness by diverting it from its purpose or weakening its ability to achieve its purpose, including, to the extent relevant to its purpose, weakening either the public's trust in that institution or the institution's inherent trustworthiness. (2013, p. 2)

For our purposes, the definition is of interest as it sheds light on legal activities and authority relationships that are working with and through established institutions and that nonetheless take advantage of and misuse the public trust[1]. One example of this, where public trust can be broken even without money changing hands, is the mere presence of ideology within an institution, such as a country's judiciary. This would remove the impartiality that the institution is meant to exercise in its judgements. The preceding definition ties in well with another issue that can be included within the 'grey zone' of the corruption debate – that is, conflict of interest. The *International Encyclopaedia of Ethics* defines 'conflict of interest' as

a situation in which some person (whether an individual or corporate body) stands in a certain relationship to one or more decisions. On the standard view, a person has a conflict of interest if, and only if, that person (1) is in a relationship with another requiring the exercise of judgement on the other's behalf and (2) has a ('secondary 'or 'unusual') interest tending to interfere with the proper exercise of such judgement.

Having a conflict of interest on its own is not wrong because such a conflict can occur easily as people act in one capacity in their private sphere and a different one in their professional sphere. The complications arise when one acts in spite of one's awareness of a conflict of interest, where one is involved. Public servants/officials hold positions of trust in the society, in the case of public administrative law, a position where they are expected to exercise their power in an impartial

---

[1] Thanks to Michael Johnston for helping us phrase it like this.

manner. However, if a conflict of interest exists in a situation and the public official chooses to exercise his or her public duty in spite of this conflict of interest and does not point out or volunteer the fact that he or she has a conflict of interest, then that public official will not be ensuring to act in an impartial manner. This results in the public official exercising his or her power in a partial manner.

The root of conflict of interest is the distortion of impartiality. A telling example of this is found in the public administrative law of Sweden, where five situations are delineated as qualifying situations for the presence of a conflict of interest:

1. If the matter concerns the person exercising judgement or anyone that he or she has a relationship with (here the examples can range from spouse, child, parent or other person considered to be a close relation) or if the execution of the case can be expected to bring benefit/harm to the person or one of his or her relations;
2. If the person or a relation holds power of attorney for the person whom the case concerns or for someone who may profit/loose from the outcome of the case;
3. If the case has been raised at an authority through appeal or other means;
4. If the person has been assigned as representative or has represented someone in exchange for commission; and
5. If over and above there are any special circumstance that would diminish the trust in the person's impartiality in the matter.

As Lessig (2013) points out, corruption is not a matter of 'good guys' and 'bad guys', where we analyze the world in black and white. The previously listed descriptions, albeit aimed at the 'output side' pertaining to civil servants, are provided as filters to differentiate between the shades of grey – and can be used at the 'input' side as well, this immediately brings into question the realm of private-sector lobbying/influence in matters of laws that affect the collective, for example, petroleum companies lobbying against the passing of environmental legislation.

## Particularism, Favouritism and Impartiality

Several authors have recently identified particularism in public policy as a central ingredient of corruption. The opposite of particularism, according to these authors, is impersonal (instead of personalistic) rule

(North et al. 2009), ethical universalism (Mungiu-Pippidi 2006) or impartiality in the exercise of public power (Rothstein and Teorell 2008). What does it mean to be impartial in the exercise of public power? Cupit (2000) writes: 'To act impartially is to be unmoved by certain sorts of considerations – such as special relationships and personal preferences. It is to treat people alike, irrespective of personal relationships and personal likes and dislikes' (cf. Barry 1995, p. 11). The connection to corruption is motivated by the fact that impartiality is the driving notion behind John Rawls' liberal 'rights-based' theory of justice. As Goodin (2004, p. 100) argues, 'Certainly, the antithesis of justice is favouritism.' In this context, impartiality is not a demand on actors on the input side of the political system but first and foremost an attribute of the actions taken by civil servants and professionals in public service, law enforcement personnel and the like (i.e. the actors on the output side).

Equally important, however, are the things that the norm of impartiality does *not* rule out. Since impartiality is a procedural norm confined to the exercise of public power, one important field that is not affected by this conception is the substance of the content of policies. This builds on the idea that non-corruption implies that 'a state ought to treat equally those who deserve equally' (Kurer 2005, p. 223). States may be unjust and ineffective, and their actions may be the result of pressure from all kinds of interest groups, but these are things that according to Rothstein and Teorell (2008) should be seen as something outside the sphere of corruption. Instead, they argue that it is impartiality in the exercise of power (the 'ought to treat equally' principle) that is the central component of what should be seen as the opposite of corruption. To treat equally does not, of course, imply that everyone should get the same. Only people who are in need of a kidney transplant should get a kidney. Instead, this follows the idea of 'equal concern and respect' launched by Ronald Dworkin (1977).

The implication is the one argued for here, namely, that impartiality cannot be a moral basis for the content of policies. What individuals, interest groups and political parties pursue on the input side of the political system may or may not be marked by Barry's (1995) reasonableness, but this is not the same as impartiality. For example, in a given situation there may be good reasons for lowering pensions and increasing support to families with children. This is, however, not the same as being impartial between these two groups because there is no such thing as an impartial way to decide in a case such as this (Arneson 1998). This is particularly problematic when it comes to conflicts over which public goods a state should provide, since such goods often cannot be divided into minor parts (like money), something that makes reasonable compromises easier to reach. Either the airport or dam is built, or nothing is built.

It is important to note that for many, increased justice implies policies that contain more partiality (e.g. extra resources to under-privileged groups). However, such people usually do not want these policies to be implemented in a partial way, where bureaucrats are given total discretion in each and every case (Tebble 2002; Young 1990). For example, it may be perfectly legitimate to argue for the government to establish academic positions that only women (or some other disadvantaged group) could apply for given the current gender inequality that exists in higher academic positions. However, once such a position is announced and a number of women apply, the impartiality norm takes overhand because those who have argued for such a quota system usually want the most qualified candidates in the preferred group to get the position. Thus, while impartiality is a norm to be followed in one sphere, it would be dysfunctional and/or also unethical in other spheres. This conditionality in the application of impartiality as a justice principle in fact goes all the way back to John Stuart Mill:

> Impartiality, in short, as an obligation of justice, may be said to mean being exclusively influenced by the considerations which it is supposed ought to influence the particular case in hand, and resisting the solicitations of any motives which prompt to conduct differently from what those considerations would dictate. (1861/1992, p. 154)

It should be underlined that the argument is not that impartiality is equivalent to 'objectivity'. Terminology is a tricky business (especially if you trade in a language that is not your own). Still we would say that, as a concept, objectivity has an absolute and perfectionist ring to it that implies that humans can have full knowledge of a case and weigh all things equally and come down to a decision as if the outcome were decided by some natural-law process. We would argue that impartiality implies somewhat more human and realistic demands. Firstly, it is about a 'matter-of-factness', implying that things that according to the policy/law should not have an impact (e.g. family connections, ethnicity or the willingness to pay a bribe) should also be left out from the decision. Secondly, it requires that the public official should not be a party to the case, neither directly nor indirectly. Moreover, the idea of impartiality as the opposite of particularism and corruption stands in sharp contrast to the public-choice idea of public officials maximizing their self-interest. For example, an impartial civil servant should not be susceptible to bribery, should not decide in cases where his or her friends and relatives are involved and should not favour any special (ethnic, economic, or any other type of organized) interest when applying laws and rules.

### Impersonal or Impartial?

Fukuyama (2014) and North et al. (2009) use the term 'impersonal' instead of the term we suggest ('impartial'). This is in all likelihood seen by these authors merely as a terminological and not a conceptual difference. However, in dictionaries, 'impersonal' is defined as 'having or showing no interest in individual people or their feelings: lacking emotional warmth',[2] or as 'without human warmth, not friendly and without features that make people feel interested or involved',[3] or as 'lacking friendly human feelings or atmosphere, making you feel unimportant'.[4] In contrast, 'impartial' is typically defined as 'not supporting one person or group more than another'[5] or as 'not prejudiced towards or against any particular side or party; fair; unbiased'.[6]

The reasons why we prefer 'impartial' to 'impersonal' is based on the notion that states, when producing public goods/services, do not only or even for the most part rely on personnel that have legal training or orientation (Fukuyama 2014, p. 95). Fukuyama also argues that this type of bureaucratic rigidity, when policies are implemented with 'no interest in individual people or their feelings', is what people usually despise about the state apparatus. Instead, both Western and developing

[2] Merriam-Webster, available at www.merriam-webster.com/dictionary/impersonal.

[3] Cambridge Dictionary Online, available at http://dictionary.cambridge.org/dictionary/english/impersonal.

[4] Oxford Dictionaries, available at www.oxforddictionaries.com/definition/learner/impersonal.

[5] Oxford Dictionaries, available at www.oxforddictionaries.com/definition/learner/impartial.

[6] Collins Dictionaries, available at www.collinsdictionary.com/dictionary/english/impartial.

states use a number of professions or semi-professions such a doctors, teachers, school principals, nurses, urban planners, architects, engineers and social workers when implementing public policies. For many of these professions, the idea that they would be working according to the 'rule of law' in the sense that they implement rules in an 'impersonal' manner makes little sense. They do, of course, follow the laws, but as is well-known from the literature about policy implementation, the laws that are supposed to guide what these professions do have to be quite general, and thus they do not entail precise information about how to handle each and every case (Hill and Hupe 2009). Instead, what is important for these groups when implementing public services are the standards, knowledge and ethics established by their professions. Moreover, we do not want nurses, teachers, people who work in elderly care or doctors to have 'no interest in individual people or their feelings' or to be 'lacking emotional warmth' when they do their jobs. On the contrary, we want them (and they usually also want) to be personally engaged in and committed to their jobs (Brante 2014, pp. 124–32). Moreover, when it comes to services that are 'human processing', they often need to fine-tune their competence so that it suites the needs of each individual case. A university professor, for example, is supposed fine-tune his or her support when supervising graduate students in accordance with the specific circumstance of the PhD project and the specific needs, competence and skills of the students. However, the professor should not let his or her private sympathies for the specific student take over so that he or she would give the student special favours. In our Swedish language, this is stated as being 'personal' but not 'private', admittedly a finely tuned but extremely important distinction.

For example, parents at the typical Danish public pre-school do not want the pre-school teacher to be 'lacking friendly human feelings' when teaching and taking care of their children. However, they would be extremely upset if they were to discover that the pre-school teachers had given special favours or treatment to some kids because their parents had paid them money under the table or because they belonged to some ethnic/religious group. The only legitimate reason they have for giving some children more attention than others is if this can be motivated by the standards established in the profession of what is good teaching and care for different children (Brante 2014, pp. 124–32). The professional groups in the state are supposed to have some autonomy/discretion to use their professional competence and judgement, but this should not be used in a way that can be deemed as giving undue favours. In other words, they should be impartial but not impersonal.

In this discussion, Fukuyama (2014) has argued that acting according to norms such as impartiality does not come naturally to humans. Instead, if given a position of power, according to Fukuyama (2014, p. 89), our 'natural inclination' is to use this power to promote our self-interest, our family, kin and clan – and one could add political faction or party. The understanding that impartiality in the exercise of public power should take precedence is thus something that must be learned through some form of public ethos. There are in fact several theoretical approaches to human behaviour that today have a strong presence in higher education and that also run counter to the ideal of impartiality. Inspired by neoclassical economics, the public-choice approach to government starts from the assumption that civil servants are operating according to the 'rent-seeking model', where agents are self-interested utility maximizers (Mueller 1997).[7] This is, of course, an axiom that is anathema to impartiality. The same can be said of most political-economic analyses built on group or class interests, whether Marxist or not. In these, the state is usually seen as an arena for the exercise of interest-based politics, which, of course, rules out the notion of impartiality (Therborn 2008). In addition, several identity-oriented approaches in which the idea that a person with identity X could make an impartial evaluation of the merits of a person with identity Y are seen as impossible (Burke and Stets 2009; Young 1990). In addition, the approach in development studies known as 'post-colonialism' understands principles such as impartiality as an expression of Western semi-imperialist ideology (de Maria 2010). In sum, the idea of defining the opposite of corruption based on the notion of impartiality is far from uncontroversial.

---

[7] This *Handbook of Public Choice* does not have index entries either for the term 'corruption' or for 'impartiality'.

# 9 | The Chinese Exception and Alternative

The starting point for this chapter is the so-called China paradox in corruption and governance research. On the one hand, as argued in Chapter 1, there is now an abundance of research in economics and political science arguing for the importance of states' administrative capacity and the quality of their government institutions for the economic prosperity and social development of countries. Corruption, in its various forms, is generally said to be detrimental to economic growth and increases in human well-being (e.g. educational attainment, access to healthcare, implementation of laws and trust in public institutions). On the other hand, the People's Republic of China (henceforth China) scores comparatively low on all commonly used measures of levels of corruption and the quality of government institutions (Bell 2015; Fukuyama 2013). Most importantly, China lacks the predictable rule-of-law–oriented and un-political type of public administration that is known as the 'Weberian model of bureaucracy' (Ahlers 2014; Birney 2013; Pieke 2009). This model for the public administration is seen by most institutional scholars as a central ingredient in the institutional setup needed to spur a country's development (Dahlström et al. 2011; Evans and Rauch 2000; North et al. 2009; Pritchett and Woolcock 2004).

Yet, as is well known, during the last three decades, China has shown exceptionally high economic growth and impressive improvements in many commonly used measures of human well-being (Sen 2011) despite its dismal performance in the available measures of levels of corruption and quality of government. The magnitude of this 'China paradox' is, for example, shown by the fact that leading scholars in the institutional approach to development have been forced to use a number of ad-hoc explanations to account for the Chinese case because the country does not fit the theory (Acemoglu and Robinson 2012, pp. 43–7; cf. Fukuyama 2012). For example, Mahbubani, as cited in Ottervik (2013, p. 22), argues that while governance in China is not perfect, it has lifted more people out of poverty, educated more people, increased their lifespans and generated the world's largest middle class. No other society in human history has improved human welfare as much as the Chinese government. It would be insane to deny that China has enjoyed 'good governance.'

Ahlers (2014, p. 1) refers to the discrepancy between the established theory about 'good governance' and what has taken place in China as 'the hardest contemporary nut that comparative political scientists have to crack'. Using Transparency International's Corruption Perception Index as a measure of institutional quality, Wedeman (2012, p. 178) shows that China is a profound outlier with a much higher annual growth rate than other countries with similar levels of corruption. However, it should be added that in this and other similar indexes, China is not ranked at the bottom and is thus not among the worst governed or most corrupt countries. Instead, China is usually just below the middle-ranked countries.

It also should be noted that despite the comparatively high levels of corruption and lack of democracy, the Chinese state has been able to increase its capacity to collect taxes, thereby being able to fund large investments in public goods such as education, health facilities and infrastructure (Ahlers 2014; Ho and Niu 2013; Ottervik 2013). Compared to almost all other communist regimes that have experienced systemic breakdowns in delivering public and private goods, as affirmed by Anna Ahlers (2014), in China, *'things are getting done'* (p. 1; italics in original). One can of course argue that in the standard comparative political science approach, where the unit of analysis usually is countries, China is just one case out of 200. This implies that in the statistics commonly used, it does not have a great impact. However, like many others, we argue that China, considering its enormous population, is quite an important case. Any theory stating that corruption and 'bad governance' are important factors behind human development can therefore not ignore the 'China paradox'. In this chapter we will present a conceptual map of how to understand what goes on in this huge and increasingly important country.

The 'puzzle of China' leaves us with three possibilities. Firstly, the theory stressing the importance of getting corruption under control and improving the quality of government institutions is a misspecification of what causes economic and social development. For example, it may be the case that the theory is not as general as the proponents argue, in the sense that it may work for some types of societies but not for others. A possible explanation is that for a country like China, low quality in its formal institutions may be compensated for by high quality in its informal institutions. For example, Li and Wu (2010) have argued that the presumably high level of interpersonal trust in China serves as an informal institutional device that mitigates the negative effects of corruption in the formal institutions. In a similar way, it has been argued that the *guanxi* networks in China not only should be seen as facilitating corruption and clientelism but also should be seen as informal systems for securing honesty in economic transactions (Huang and Wang 2011; Li 2011). The problem with these explanations is that they imply that China can only be explained by referring to cultural and historical traits that are specific to China, such as the legacy of Confucianism (Bell 2015). This may very well be true, but from a comparative perspective, there are strong arguments for trying to find a more general explanation for the 'China puzzle'. Otherwise, comparative politics may end up with one theory of development per country. Before retracting to the 'culturalist' type of explanation, there are good reasons to see if it is possible to find a more universal explanation for the China paradox.

A second possibility is that there is something profoundly wrong with how corruption and the quality of government institutions is conceptualized by the group of mostly Western scholars who are engaged in this topic and that this is specifically detrimental to the Chinese case. A central issue here is, of course, the relation between universalism and cultural relativism in the social sciences. The latter approach would argue that concepts such as 'good governance', 'corruption' and the 'quality of government' are based on profoundly Western ideals and therefore should not be applied to other cultures such as China. As we argued earlier and will show in Chapter 10, several studies show that there is not much empirical support for this relativistic approach (Persson et al. 2013; Rothstein & Torsello 2014; Widmalm 2005). A third possibility is that there is some kind of institutional feature in the Chinese system of governing that has been left out of the discussion. If so, this would imply that state capacity and quality of government can be reached by other means than the liberal, rule-of-law–based Weberian model of state capacity as first put forward by Evans and Rauch (2000).

We will concentrate on the latter issue because our inclination is that the institutional theory of development probably is right. To summarize, we think that both the internal logic of the institutional theory and the results from many different types of empirical research are to this day convincing. The assumption from which this analysis starts is that 'the problem with China' may be related to a misunderstanding of the main operational mode of Chinese public administration. The hypothesis put forward is that research on this topic may have missed the importance of a specific organizational form of public administration, namely, the 'cadre organization'. It is argued that this quite specific type of public administration is conceptually a very different organizational species from the Weberian model based on rule of law and impartial bureaucracy. However, as will be shown, this cadre type of public administration is *not* a specific Chinese model of public administration because, while rare, it can also be found in Western democracies. This implies that high-quality government and control of corruption can be reached by other means than by Weberian impartial rule-of-law institutions. Most importantly, it is argued that for producing socially efficient outcomes, due to its specific organizational form, this cadre model of public administration can under some circumstances be more efficient than the Weberian model. The implication thus is that in singling out the rule-of-law, impartial and politically neutral Weberian model as a requirement for successful development, the institutional approach in economics and political science may have been mistaken.

## Measuring the Quality of Government in China

Despite fairly high levels of corruption and far from ideal implementation, the Chinese population seems to be quite satisfied with government services in general (Ahlers 2014). Comparing six large Asian-Pacific countries, Wang (2010) showed that Chinese citizens are more content with how their government handles issues such as crime, unemployment, human rights, the economy, political corruption and improving the quality of public services than citizens in countries such as Japan, Russia, India and the United States. In this study, only Australia outperformed China.

Data from the World Value Study survey carried out in 2007 show that not only does China have markedly higher levels of social trust and

**Table 9.1** *Generalized Trust, Confidence in Institutions and Economic Growth*

|  | China | Peru | India | Morocco | Brazil | Mexico |
|---|---|---|---|---|---|---|
| Generalized trust (%) | 52.3 | 6.3 | 23.3 | 13 | 9.4 | 15.6 |
| Confidence in institutions (%) |  |  |  |  |  |  |
| Police | 80.1 | 15.8 | 64.1 | 61.4 | 44.8 | 33.6 |
| Civil services | 85.8 | 6 | 54.3 | 51.3 | 52.4 | 25 |
| Gross domestic product (GDP) growth (%) | 9.1 | 5.02 | 3.77 | 3.32 | 2.66 | 0.83 |
| GDP per capita growth (%) | 8.37 | 3.55 | 2.17 | 2.09 | 1.25 | −0.19 |

*Source:* Quality of Government (QoG) Dataset; see Teorell et al. (2013).

higher growth rates than other large developing countries – despite that they all resemble each other when it comes to their levels of corruption, as shown in Table 9.1. However, the Chinese population seems to have substantially higher confidence in the police and the civil service.

One possible conclusion from these figures is that while corruption and corruption-related problems may be common, there is something else in the Chinese state that creates the high confidence in public institutions among the population. The question is, what? Ahlers and Schubert (2011, p. 66) suggest that political legitimacy at the local level in China is secured by what they label 'adaptive authoritarianism', which implies that the local cadres have an obligation to 'to be aware of public demands (including beliefs and values) and thus take into account the people's responses to the policy'. The importance of the high levels of confidence in the public administration and police should also be seen in relation to a number of survey-based comparative studies about political legitimacy in general. What these studies show is that issues that relate to the 'output side' of the political system, such as government effectiveness and control of corruption, are generally more important for creating political legitimacy among the population than are the standard set of liberal democratic rights (Dahlberg and Holmberg 2014; Gilley 2006; Gjefsen 2012).

The central question, then, is, how is this done? As a starting point, it is important to note that the term 'civil servant' cannot be directly imported from the English language to translate to the same understanding in Chinese. In China, the term for civil servant covers both party cadre and non-party government officials, which implies that it is difficult to separate the term because it encompasses, in practical terms, more than one job category (Chou 2008). A first implication of this is that the central notion of the model of Weberian bureaucracy (i.e. that civil servants are not to be loyal to the ruling political party, but instead their loyalty is to the rule-of-law principles and their professional standards) does not apply to China (Pieke 2009).

## Reforming the Civil Service in China

Recent scholarship on the Chinese civil service has focused on the many and encompassing civil service reforms initiated by the Deng leadership in the 1980s and later reinvigorated in 1993 (Burns 2007; Burns and Wang 2010; Keping 2014; Pieke 2009), as well as on the legal framework that serves as the basis and starting point to institutionalize these reforms. A central finding in the literature about the civil service in China is that there is still an overwhelming presence of the Communist Party within the civil service (Ahlers 2014; Bell 2015; Burns 2007; Burns and Wang 2010; Burns and Zhiren 2010; Chou 2008; Collins and Chan 2009; Heberer and Göbel 2011; Ledberg 2014; Liou et al. 2012; Pieke 2009). The extent of the party's involvement is demonstrated by the fact that a member of the Politburo's seven-member Standing Committee is in charge of overseeing organization and personnel work, including management of the civil service. The fact that party members make up 80 per cent of civil service posts, in the roughly five and a half million–strong civil service (Burns 2007), is evidence of the civil service being dominated by the ruling Communist Party. It also reinforces the absence of a Weberian-style 'civil service neutrality' in the Chinese public administration (Birney 2013; Burns 2007). However, the influence of the Communist Party is in line with Wedeman's explanation for the 'China paradox', namely, that the centrally launched anti-corruption campaigns, while not making China into Denmark, have had a considerable effect in preventing corruption to spiral out of control (Bell 2015; Wedeman 2012; cf. Gong 2011).

While party control is still very important, China has made strong efforts to increase the levels of professionalism, meritocracy, skills and educational requirement in its public administration (Bell 2015, p. 185; Ho and Niu 2013; Keping 2014; Pieke 2009; cf. Ledberg 2014). In 1993, admission criteria to the civil service were revised as part of the reform, to include university degrees as part of the selection process. By 2003, the civil service reforms had shown significant improvement in the quality of its civil servants, with 70 per cent of civil servants having university degrees (Burns and Wang 2010). The competition for jobs in the central administration is very high (Bell 2015, p. 185; Ho and Niu 2013). According to one study, in 2009, more than 775,000 applicants competed for some 13,500 jobs (Burns and Zhiren 2010).

During the pre-reform era, evaluation of civil servants rested strongly on one single criterion, namely, party loyalty (Chou 2008; Pieke 2009). However, beginning in the early 1990s, this seems to have shifted towards a strong emphasis on the actual performance of civil service to deliver services (Bell 2015; Burns and Zhiren 2010; Chen 2005; Edin 2003, 2005; Gao 2009). Starting at the county and township levels in the early 1990s, 'performance and results based management' has, according to Burns and Zhiren (2010), Gao (2009) and Edin (2003), become a central model for the implementation of public policy in China. In this model, which according to Gao (2009, p. 22) has been overlooked in most studies of state capacity in China, government authorities at higher levels are setting increasingly precise and quantifiable targets for the administration at regional, county and township levels to which individual civil servants also are held accountable (Edin 2003, p. 36). It can be argued that this should be seen as a systematic strengthening of state capacity by increasing 'institutional adaptability' at the local level (see also Ahlers 2014; Gao 2009; Keping 2014). One effect is that the careers of public officials have been increasingly tied to how well they are able to fulfil specific policy mandates (Birney 2013). Some of these performance targets, such as family planning, social security and handling of mass protests, have been tied directly to individual civil servants and have carried powerful sanctions if not met (Burns and Zhiren 2010, p. 15; Edin 2003). According to one study based on interviews with county officials, such targets 'were the most important task for leadership cadres, and the accomplishment of targets ... brought great pressure for local officials, especially for cadres in the leadership corps who were directly accountable' (Gao, cited in Burns and Zhiren 2010, p. 16). What is particularly interesting is that the performance targets at the county and township levels are a mix of ideological, political, economic, educational and social goals. Examples given by Gao, cited in Burns and Zhiren (2010, pp. 18ff; see also Heberer and Göder 2011, p. 37), include

- Building party branches in resident communities;
- At least 80 per cent of 'women's diseases' should be under control;
- Making a practical plan for dealing with mass complaints;
- Ensuring that 95 per cent of social conflicts are handled by means of negotiation;
- Ensuring an annual growth rate of $x$ per cent;
- Reduction of water consumption by $x$ per cent;
- Population reduction by $x$ per cent; and
- Conduct of moral education among the youth.

The policy goals distributed to each area are prioritized in a certain order as well, where the highest-priority goal is given most attention because it reflects on the performance of the individual civil servant. In a case where the top-priority goal is not advanced according to the set target but other goals from the list have in fact been achieved, the civil servants' overall 'score' assigned by the central administration will be lowered. Such a mix of ideological and policy goals and the 'scoreboard' of civil servants neither resemble what is to be expected from a Western-style rule-of-law-based politically neutral, impartial Weberian bureaucracy. What is especially interesting is that economic and social efficiency goals are being mixed with ideological goals such as 'conducting moral education', something that would be alien for a Weberian type of public administration (cf. Pieke 2009). The question is whether we can find a model for public administration that fits a list of such diverging types of goals? One explanation is provided by Birney (2013), who labels this system 'rules by mandates'. She argues that this system is fundamentally different from a rule-of-law system because the mandates, unlike laws, are hierarchically ordered, meaning that the administration is supposed to disregard a 'lower' mandate if its implementation, in the specific local context, stands in the way of carrying out a mandate with higher priority (Birney 2013, p. 56). Moreover, while laws are public, many of the mandates governing public administration in China are often secret, especially the internal ranking of the mandates. In sum, the reformed public administration model in China differs from the traditional

Communist model in that in addition to party loyalty and ideological coherence, since about 1990 there has also been a strong emphasis on competence, education and performance to deliver services (Bell 2015, p. 185; Pieke 2009).

## Public Administration and Development under Authoritarian Regimes

While China must be characterized as a non-democratic authoritarian regime, not all such regimes are the same. In a comparative study of seventy-six countries using data from 1983–2003, Charron and Lapuente (2011) differentiated between three types of authoritarian regimes, namely, single-party regimes, monarchies, and military/personalistic rule. Using a variety of measures for quality of government (QoG), they found substantial differences in the level of QoG among these types of authoritarian rule. Single-party regimes have the highest level of QoG when economic prosperity is taken into account. Their argument is that at a modest level of economic prosperity, single-party regimes are much better than monarchies or military regimes in channelling demands from citizens into higher levels of state capacity. This is also shown in recent empirical research on governing in China. Included in the performance-based-mandate style of management system are systematic demands on local officials to measure (by surveys) citizens' satisfaction with various policies and with 'government work style, integrity and clean government' (Burns and Zhiren 2010, p. 21; cf. Edin 2003). It is noteworthy that the existence of performance-based management is neither confined to nor has its origin in China. Instead, as Gao (2009) showed, it has originated in and is often practiced in the West. For example, in 1995, the Organisation for Economic Co-operation and Development (OECD) published a report entitled, 'Performance Management in Governance: Performance, Measurement and Result-Oriented Management', in which this form of public administration was highly recommended. What is special about the Chinese performance-based management is that soft ideological and hard professional targets are mixed (Ahlers 2014; Birney 2013).

How this works is shown also in a study of how the system for regulating banks works in China (He 2014). While formal rules exist, most of the regulation is done informally by direct verbal or telephone communication from the China Banking Regulation Commission to the banks telling them, for example, what sectors to increase or decrease lending to and to 'signal risks to the financial institutions'. These instructions are 'never in writing'. Instead, this steering from the centre is described as 'suasive' and 'allow[s] the regulator to respond to constantly changing conditions without the need for frequent formal amendments'. This allows for a constant interaction between the regulating authority and the banks for implementing a 'tailored approach for regulating different categories of banks in terms of size and complexity'. This steering by persuasion instead of rules does not rely on any 'legal or binding regulatory consequences' or 'explicit penalty sanctions' (He 2014, pp. 65ff). Instead, according to He (2014, p. 67), what makes this system work is 'paternalistic' persuasion.

In sum, China has dramatically increased the educational demands for and professional competence of its civil service, but the Communist Party is still heavily in control. Demands on performance and accountability have increased, as have efforts to measure citizens' satisfaction with performance. However, this mode of governing is not based on the impartial and politically neutral Weberian rule-of-law model. On the contrary, the aforementioned empirical studies, not least the detailed ethnographic study based on numerous interviews with students and teachers at the party schools by Pieke (2009), as well as the study of the rural administration by Ahlers (2014), strongly support the existence of a very different organizational modus operandi in the Chinese public administration. This is a system in which performance goals and hierarchically ordered mandates are set centrally, giving local cadres fairly large discretionary power over how to reach the targets – what Edin (2003, p. 36) labels 'institutional adaptability' reminiscent of the leeway afforded to civil servants in accordance with their professional norms. This may be judged as a volatile policy process, but on the flip side, it provides a shorter turnover, where the discretion of civil servants not only helps to adapt policy to the local settings but also provides a more or less instantaneous feedback mechanism to the central administration (indicating whether a policy is in need of change). A central conclusion is that 'state capacity' in China is organized in a way that is very different from the Weberian model rule-of-law type of 'good government' launched in the institutional development theory. The question is whether we can find a general theory or model of public administration and state capacity that makes sense of this without resorting to a culturalist China-specific explanation for how to understand what is to be seen as state capacity and quality of government.

## The Cadre Organization and the China Paradox

The hypothesis we will present is that the puzzle of why China has thrived despite what has been perceived as low quality of government may be found in the interface between the ruling Communist Party and the public administration. Our hypothesis is that the combination of single-party rule and the type of reforms of the public administration described earlier may have resulted in an organizational form for China's public administration that works as a solution to the most general problem in organizational theory, implementation research and public administration, namely, the issue of how to handle 'delegated discretion'.

The literature on public administration is sometimes steeped in the language of economics, in which the goals of the principals are clear, and the agents are rational utility-oriented self-interested types. Here the major problem is how the principal can create an incentive structure that makes it rational for his or her agents to strive to achieve the goals of the organization instead of engaging themselves in all kinds of fraudulent and self-serving actions. As shown by Gary Miller, for example, if the tasks that are going to be performed by the agents are complex, the rational choice type of incentive steering cannot work. The reason is that the principal, in order to create the right type of incentive system, needs correct information from the agents about the work process. However, if the agents think that the principal will use this information against their interest, for example, by increasing their work efforts, they will not reveal such correct information, which will make it impossible for the principal to set correct incentives (Miller 1992). This asymmetry information problem makes it impossible to steer organizations in the mechanical way that rational choice theory presumes – if this is tried, the organization is likely to fall into a situation known as a 'social trap', where everyone involved will lose because of the lack of mutual trust (Rothstein 2005). In corruption research, this principal-agent theory represents a serious misspecification of the problem because it relies on the existence of 'the honest principal'. However, in a situation characterized by systemic corruption, we should expect the actors at the top, that is, the principal, to earn most of the rents from corruption. The implication is that such principals will have no incentive to change the incentive structure for corrupt agents (Persson et al. 2013).

This rational-choice-based theory of organization has been successfully challenged by a more cultural approach. In this model, scholars rightly stress the importance of commonly held beliefs, mutual trust, informal norms, communicative leadership and so on (Ashkanasy et al. 2011; Miller 1992). The problem here is that any notion of even a semi-rational steering of the organization to a set of goals, such as improving the economy and social welfare of a country, tends to get lost. One widely held view, in this approach to organizations and public administration systems, sees such systems as 'garbage cans' to which uncoordinated streams of problems, solutions, participants and choice opportunities flow, creating an anarchic situation that cannot be governed in any meaningful sense of the word (Cohen et al. 1972).

Although not often discussed in organization and management theory or in theories of public administration, there is an alternative form of public administration that avoids the pitfalls of the two aforementioned models. It can be described as an 'ideal type' in the same manner as the well-known Weberian ideal type of the politically neutral legalistic bureaucracy. A useful term for this organizational type is the 'cadre organization' (Balla 1972; Therborn 2008; cf. Rothstein 1996), also known, by management scholars, as the 'missionary model' (Mintzberg 2010) or the 'clan model' (Ouchi 1980). This type of organization of the public administration has a rationale that is fundamentally different not only from the economic-incentive-driven model and anarchic 'garbage can' culture-based model but also from the Weberian bureaucratic ideal type. The cadre organization is based on steering by neither formal and/or precise rules, any rule-of-law conception of tasks, nor economic incentives. Instead, the basis for this organization is a strong ideologically based commitment from the personnel (the cadre) to the specific 'policy doctrine' of the organization. As opposed to the Weberian bureaucrat's neutral *sine ira et studio*[1] orientation, the cadre is characterized by his or her strong loyalty to or even passion for the policy doctrine of the organization. The cadre's key skill is the ability to understand and embrace the organization's policy doctrine and to implement this doctrine

---

[1] Latin; translation is not easy but should be something like 'without anger or passion'.

in varying circumstances, in which the tools used are constantly adapted to the specific circumstances at hand. The difference between cadre and Weberian bureaucrats is not primarily in their level of professionalism, education and skills but in what these are used for and *how*. The cadre organization can be based on as much professionalism as the bureaucratic organization, but the skills are applied according to a very different logic. In an early and remarkable work on this topic, Hungarian-German sociologist Balint Balla described the difference between the bureaucratic and cadre organizations in the following way:

While bureaucracy is characterized by reliability, continuity, efficacy, precise application of prevailing instructions ... cadre administration is marked ... by flexible immediate 'line-oriented' dynamism, by superiority over formalities and pragmatic ability to adjust to changing situations. (Balla 1972, from Therborn 2008, p. 137)

For understanding the role of the cadre organization model in contemporary China, it is important to emphasize that while it can certainly be driven by adherence to an ideological doctrine (e.g. Marxism-Leninism), this is not a necessary condition. As will be shown later, instead of being grounded on a political ideology, the cadre model can also be based on adherence to specific policy in, for example, healthcare, education or demography. Thus, while the importance of the Marxist-Leninist ideology seems to have faded in China, this has not made the cadre model of public administration less relevant (Ledberg 2014; Pieke 2009; cf. Bell 2015).

## The Cadre Organization in Western Societies

Empirically, the cadre model of public administration just described is not confined to a specific culturally based Chinese or Communist mode of public administration. In fact, mainstream organizational theorists in the West have made occasional references to this organizational form. For example, in his well-known taxonomy of organizations, Henry Mintzberg mentioned the existence of what he called the 'missionary organization' (Mintzberg 2010). Likewise, William Ouchi identified what he labelled the 'clan organization' (Ouchi 1980). More recent analysis of the 'mission type' of public administration has verified the existence and importance of ideological motivation for policy doctrines among civil servants (Wright et al. 2012).

Although rarely theorized by public administration scholars, this type of organization has been empirically verified in countries that are very different from contemporary China, such as the United States and Sweden.

A case in point is a 'modern classic' in public administration from the United States, namely, Herbert Kaufman's study of the Forest Service published in 1960 (Kaufman 1960). In this book, *The Forest Ranger*, Kaufman describes the severe problem of how to apply the quite loose laws and regulations to the 792 different districts that the Forest Service was responsible for. Since they could not be supervised in any meaningful way, Kaufman asks why the district rangers he studied did not de facto implement 792 different policies. The answer he came up with is largely in line with the cadre organization model. Kaufman stressed the importance of leadership for the creation of a common ideological orientation in the organization. The methods used by the leaders of the Forest Service involved: 1) recruiting persons strongly inclined to the type of work that was to be done; 2) using extensive internal training to nurture 'the will to conform' to the organization's goals, and; 3) organizing the work so that the will by the Rangers to identify with the Forest Service was strengthened. 'Without realizing it', wrote Kaufman, 'members of the Forest Service thus internalize the perceptions, values, and premises of action that prevail in the bureau, unconsciously, very often, they tend to act in the agency-prescribed fashion because that has become natural to them' (Kaufman 1960, 162, 171, 176). In this way, the Forest Service in the United States turned out to be very successful in handling the problem of delegated authority.

Another example can be taken from implementation of the 'active labour market policy' (ALMP) in Sweden starting in the 1950s. This policy was created by two economists from the blue-collar union federation (Gösta Rehn and Rudolf Meidner). Their idea was that the unions, in order to increase unity and avoid inflationary wage demands, should strive for a universal (solidaristic) wage policy. This would imply that individual companies as well as whole sectors of the economy making low profits would pay wages at the same level as those who had high profits. Instead of fighting against economic rationalization what would put less profitable industries out of work, the unions should embrace this development because it would increase economic growth since capital and labour would flow to the more expansive sectors. The problem was of course how to take care of and compensate workers that were laid off because of this policy. The policy doctrine, known as the Rehn-Meidner model, was that through 'active' measures, such as extensive vocational training, highly qualified job finding services, and generous support for relocation, laid-off workers should be moved to the more profitable and successful areas of the economy. However, the proponents of this (then quite unique) economic model realized that this would not be an easy task to implement since many workers would be reluctant to change location and type of work. In order to handle this problem, a new type of 'cadre' administration was established known as the National Board for Labour Market Policy. Recruitment of personnel to this organization, not least it's street level organization, the labour exchanges, were in practice reserved for people with experience as local union officials. Their argument was that this was needed in order to get legitimacy in the implementation process from the 'target group' because people with a background in the union movement had been 'walking the walk and could talk the talk'. This was repeatedly underscored by the model's proponents that the organization was not to be governed by strict rules and regulations. Instead, it was given a large discretion and freedom in how to apply its extensive funds to the varying local and industrial specific circumstances. The schooling and training of the 'cadres' was extensive and consisted as creating understanding and support for the specific policy doctrine.

The implementation problem was of course that each individual worker who became unemployed through this massive structural economic transformation had very specific capabilities for handling the situation. Some could be re-educated through various forms of vocational training, but others not. Some could be persuaded to move to another location, but for others this was not a possible solution. Some just needed assistance to search for new work and should get temporary unemployment insurance while doing so. And some would be more suitable for various forms of temporary relief work that would be set up and administrated by the Labour Market Board. In reality, the measures had to almost be tailored for each person, which in many cases included a fair amount of persuasion. It was obvious for policymakers that solving this riddle through a rule-bound and legal type of Weberian steering would have been impossible and would have resulted in a bureaucratic nightmare that would have severely delegitimized the whole policy. Instead, they created a cadre organization to solve this by customizing the 'active' measures according to the specific needs and capabilities of each individual in accordance with the overall goal of this policy doctrine. The organization was deliberately infused with a strong ideological commitment to the policy/doctrine through various educational, social and cultural measures (Milner and Wadensjö 2001; Rothstein 1996).

What took place in the ALMP in Sweden during its heyday in the 1960s and 1970s looks remarkably similar to how the local administrative cadre rule–by-mandate system works in China when deciding which local companies to support. When the traditional central planning system was abandoned in the early 1990s, it was replaced by 'active industrial policies', where the local cadres were given the responsibility to decide which companies to support by 'concentrating local resources on strategic key enterprises'. General policies were set at the national level, but it was up to the local cadres to 'pick the winners'. Instead of central decisions on what products to produce, the local cadres had to decide which companies could become economically successful (Edin 2005, pp. 112–14). The success of the local cadres was, of course, monitored, and they were held accountable, but they did not operate through a set of central rules or regulations. According to Edin (2005, p. 117), this is known as the 'cadre responsibility system', in which 'soft' ideological targets could often be as important as 'hard' production targets. Among the former could also be such things as handling protests, securing social order and preventing environmental problems.

While the Weberian bureaucratic rule-of-law model has many advantages, not least in its predictability, process-bound qualities and meritocratic recruitment, the cadre organization has at least one feature that can be particularly important in a very large and rapidly developing country. The studies referred to earlier show that this type of organization is particularly apt to solve the aforementioned 'delegation problem' in organizational theory. It is well known in public administration research, especially in research about implementation of social and educational reforms, that the rule-of-law model is difficult to apply in many areas where there is a need to adapt the interventions to the specific circumstances of the case (for an overview, see Rothstein 1998, chap. 4). There are a number of ways in which this can be solved, for example, by using staff with a strong professional knowledge about what to do in such cases (e.g. like medical doctors handling patients with bacterial infections). However, for many public policies, for example, in areas such as education, social work, industrial policy and urban planning, such applicable professional knowledge does not exist, but the principal still has to allow for a wide degree of discretion by agents if they are going to be able to perform their tasks (as was the case with the Forest Service in the United States).

The potential to solve the delegation problem in areas such as these with increased rule-of-law types of regulations is in fact minimal. If this is attempted, the layer of rules and regulations will become so complex that it works against predictability and increases the problem of delegated discretion (Rothstein 1998, chap. 4). However, the cadre type of organization is meant to solve this complicated steering problem. When it works, the ideological commitment and training of the cadre in the general policy doctrine handle the problem of delegated discretion because *the agents will choose the measures that the principal would have applied in the specific situation if the principal would have had the same information about the case as the agent has.* This is why the cadre organization relies much more on internal ideological schooling than merits from outside training or from work outside the organizations when staff are recruited and promoted. Simply put, faced with a new and unprecedented case, the cadre agent is supposed to do what the principal would have done for promoting the policy doctrine had he or she 'been there'.

## Comparing the Weberian Bureaucracy and the Cadre Organization

While it is true, as stated by the cultural school in organization theory, that norms play a central part in organizations, this does not imply that organizations should generally be understood as 'garbage cans', to which norms flow in an unregulated and uncoordinated manner. In the cadre organization model, as just illustrated, the norms (or mandates) are manufactured 'from above', giving a high level of stability and coordination to the organization. This cadre organization approach has the advantage of not conflating the importance of norms in organizations with making what the organizations do indeterminate (Fukuyama 2004, p. 65). On the contrary, in the cadre type of organization, the strong concentration on the importance of ideological commitment to a specific policy doctrine, be it how to preserves national forests, get the unemployed back to work, teach students science or chose which small companies have the best future, is meant to make norms determine action at the point of implementation (cf. Pieke 2009). Another advantage of the cadre organization is that its personnel are usually trained to rapidly follow changes of operative ideology that come from the top. While the policy doctrine is general, implementation of the doctrine will usually have to vary depending on the specific circumstances. In sum, in a rapidly changing society, in which interventions under uncertain and varying conditions are needed, this may be the most important advantage the cadre model has compared with both the Weberian bureaucracy and the economic-incentive-based type of organization. The reason why corruption is controlled (though definitively not erased) and that the state manages to implement policies successfully is that the induced loyalty to the specific policy doctrine serves as a powerful counterforce against corrupt behaviour.

From the viewpoint of representative democracy, however, the cadre organization is clearly problematic because the very idea of representative democracy is that a new majority should also result in important shifts in various policy doctrines. For a cadre organization, this spells problems because its personnel may be so strongly committed to the previous majority's policy doctrine that it cannot or will not change.[2] However, this problem does not occur in a non-democratic country such as China. From a liberal rights perspective, another disadvantage of the cadre organization is that citizens and private companies cannot predict government actions because they are not rule bound. For example, in his analysis of banking regulation in contemporary China, He (2014, p. 49) pointed out that foreign (i.e., Western) banks have a hard time understanding the type of informal steering that is used by the central regulatory agency.

The cadre type of public administration should not be conflated with a politicized public administration in which positions are given to people in exchange for political support. Neo-patrimonial clientelism and US-style 'spoils' systems are different because for the cadre administration it is

---

2  An example of this can be taken from the Swedish International Development Cooperation Agency, which for a very long time had been steeped in a policy doctrine shaped by the Swedish Social Democratic Party. When in 2006 a conservative-led government took power that adhered to a quite different policy doctrine based on how international aid should be carried out, this created a lot of turbulence in the organization.

**Table 9.2** *Characteristics of Bureaucratic and Cadre Organizations*

| Characteristic | Bureaucracy | Cadre |
| --- | --- | --- |
| Recruitment | Formal merits | Commitment |
| Internal steering | Universal rules | Policy doctrine/mandates |
| Formal control | Substantial | Negligible |
| Operational logic | Legal rationality | Performance rationality |
| External relations | Predictable | Change oriented |
| Internal cohesion | Weak | Strong |
| Leadership style | Rule oriented | Mission oriented |
| Relation to clients | Neutral | Persuasive |
| Motivation | Incentives | Fulfilment of mandates |
| Tools | Routine | Flexible |

support and the ability to perform according to a specific policy doctrine that is paramount. The strong emphasis on loyalty and central control over implementation of the system of hierarchically ordered mandates may also explain why the anti-corruption campaigns stressed by Wedman (2012) have not been without success. The difference between the Weberian bureaucracy and the cadre organization can be summarized as in Table 9.2 (from Rothstein 1996, p. 31).

It follows that the cadre is not impartial or politically neutral in the same manner as the Weberian bureaucrat because fulfiling the (often shifting) specific goals, which are derived from the organization's general policy doctrine, is the primary norm. However, this is not to say that impartiality is irrelevant for the cadre (as for the professional) at another and more basic level. While the cadre is not supposed to be neutral in relation to the policy doctrine, he or she is not supposed to sway away from implementing this doctrine because of bribes, prejudices against ethnic or other minorities or engagement in nepotism or clientelism. In the two Western cases mentioned earlier (the US Forest Service and the Swedish National Labour Market Authority), corruption seemed to have been almost non-existent. On the contrary, the cadres in both these public administrations seem to have been models of loyalty and honesty.

The same type of impartiality seems to exist for professionals in many public organizations. Doctors, nurses, pre-school teachers and social workers are not supposed to act as neutral rule-of-law Weberian bureaucrats when deciding how to deal with their 'cases'. Instead, the presumption is that they should be able not only to differentiate their actions according to the specific needs of each and every case but also to show emphatic skills. However, they are not supposed to differentiate their efforts depending on bribes, personal connections, political leanings or ethnic or racial prejudices. The ability of cadres and professionals to differentiate their efforts without making considerations that may influence the case (e.g. the factors mentioned earlier) can be thought of as a 'second-order impartiality'.

As is well known, both the Weberian bureaucratic type of organization and the cadre organization can go astray. Balla (1972, from Therborn 2008, p. 139) stated that while the former can also be characterized by 'pedantry, formalism, red tape and ... trained incapacity', the cadre organization can be marked by 'dilettantism, amorphous aversion to responsibility, rigid authoritarianism, rule-resistance, incompetence and emotional paternalism'. Our point is thus not to make a normative argument for one or the other but to emphasize that a high level of economic growth and increased human well-being can be reached not only by the Weberian type of rule-of-law-oriented neutral bureaucracy but also by the cadre type of ideologically driven organization. The moderate-to-high level of corruption that according to various measures exist in China is in all likelihood real, but the negative effects of this may be compensated for by the effectiveness of the cadre type of administration.

## The Chinese Alternative: Some Conclusions

The starting point for this chapter was the well-known 'China paradox' in institutional theories about development, which is the lack of explanation for why the country has been able to show such remarkable economic growth and increases in the measures of human well-being while at the same time, according to available measures, having both relatively high corruption and a lack of the type of neutral Weberian public administration said to be necessary for reaching such goals. The hypothesis we have to put forward for how to understand this puzzle is that when assessing the quality of government in China, the stark focus on rule of law and the lack of Weberianism seems to have overlooked the existence of a possible alternative to these two institutions. This alternative may be a specific type of public administration known as the 'cadre' (or 'clan' or 'missionary') organizational model. As has been shown, this type organization has an operational logic that is fundamentally different from that of the Weberian bureaucracy. Moreover, this organization can be very efficient at producing highly valued outcomes, and it may thereby increase the system's overall political legitimacy. It should be underlined that this type of organization, while usually overlooked both in general public administration research and in comparative political science and development research, is not a result of a specific Chinese administrative culture, since it has also existed in Western countries. Compared to the neutral Weberian bureaucracy, it is likely to perform better in highly flexible terrains because it is better suited to deal with the famous delegation problem in organizations. This also implies that by leaving out the features of the cadre organization model, the available standard measures of QoG and corruption in China may be inadequate. However, a major drawback of the cadre model is, of course, that it is not very compatible with representative democracy because the latter implies that the policy doctrines that are to be implemented should change when the political majority changes. However, this is not a problem for contemporary China.

One remaining issue concerns the sustainability of the cadre model of development in China. In their widely read book, *Why Nations Fail*, Acemoglu and Robinson (2012, p. 442) predict that China will soon crash because its lack of 'inclusive' and rule-of-law types of institutions. The problem with their analysis is the lack of attention to the public administration side of the equation. As shown earlier, what goes on at the 'output' side of the political system has been shown empirically to be most important for creating political legitimacy. The efficiency of the cadre model may contribute to the overall sustainability of the Chinese model of governing despite its lack of 'inclusive' political institutions. Another question is, of course, whether the increasing economic, intellectual and political interactions with countries in which the Weberian model dominates eventually may force China to abandon the cadre model. Our guess is that as long as the Communist Party will be able to keep its dominating position, there is not much that speaks for a radical change in the modus operandi of the country's public administration. On the contrary, the cadre model seems to be very well entrenched in the system for recruitment and training (Keping 2014; Pieke 2009) as well as in the general perception of what is to be expected from a public official (Ahlers 2014). However, if the country were to change to a two- or multiparty democracy, the days of the cadre model probably would be minimal.

# 10 | *In Conclusion: What Is the Opposite of Corruption?*

## The Problem with Governance

As stated in Chapter 1, the concept of 'good governance' has been introduced, in part, as a code phrase for the opposite of corruption. A central conceptual problem in this discussion is that there are at least three very different ideas of what constitutes 'governance' in the social sciences. The first has its background mainly in the public administration and public policy analysis of Western democracies. Its basis was the recognition, beginning in the early 1990s, that an increasing number of empirical studies have shown that Western democracies no longer rely mainly on government authorities when trying to reach public or collective goals. It was argued that traditional public administration structures that used to have a monopoly, or at least were the main actor, in implementing public policies had been weakened, replaced or challenged by various forms of public-private partnerships and more loose networks of organizations, including various civil society organizations, trade organizations and private companies (Pierre 2000). The empirical studies showed that various forms of market solutions were also used for providing what were essentially public goods, such as, for example, publicly financed charter school systems and pseudo-market systems in the provision of healthcare. This development was seen as a result of a long-standing critique in Western democracies of the traditional Weberian type of public administration as being 'rigid and bureaucratic, expensive and inefficient' (Pierre and Peters 2005, p. 5).

The critique of the Weberian model of bureaucracy as not being able to function well for the more interventionist and 'human-processing' public policies has been almost endless (du Gay 2000; Rothstein 1998). In this line of research and theory, governance is seen as a society's pursuit of collective goals through various forms of steering and coordination, independent of the formal status of the actors involved

(Levi-Faur 2012; Pierre and Peters 2000). Normatively, as well as empirically, in large parts of this approach to governance, which we prefer to label as the 'policy approach' to governance, the main idea was built on a critique of the classical Weberian model of public administration. The critique pointed at the fact that this top-down steering of public administration lacked participatory elements and was incapable of handling the types of complex implementation tasks that modern Western societies were in need of. Especially what came to be known as 'implementation research' showed a number of pathological trends when central policy ambitions and programmes met reality on the ground (Rothstein 1998, chap. 3). Under umbrella terms such as 'new public administration', both more market-oriented governance systems and more network and participatory systems were supposed to provide more flexibility and increased adaption of steering measures to a more demanding and competition-oriented society (Lynn 2012). A large part of this literature also argued that the public administration should use more competition- and performance-based measures imported from the private sector (Laegreid and Christensen 2007).

This post-Weberian policy approach to governance has become a fairly large enterprise, judged by the number of publications and citations (Levi-Faur 2012). For example, it almost completely dominates the recently published 800-page *Oxford Handbook of Governance*. The index of this handbook has only five entries about 'corruption' but fifty about 'participatory governance' and forty-eight on 'network governance'. The same can be seen in the only international academic journal titled *Governance* – searching for the term 'management' in abstracts yields five times as many articles than a search on 'corruption'. It also should be noted that this approach to governance rarely concerns issues about the public administration in developing countries (Pierre and Rothstein 2011)

The problem is that the conceptualization of governance in this approach is not overwhelmingly precise. On the contrary, leading governance scholars tend to make a virtue of conceptual ambiguity. An example is David Levi-Faur (2012, p. 3), who, in his introductory chapter in the *Oxford Handbook of Governance* mentioned earlier, states that this publication intends to demonstrate that 'governance is increasingly becoming a broad concept that is central to the study of political, economic, spatial and social order in general'. In a critical analysis, Claus Offe (2009) has pointed to the fact that the concept is empty of agency. There is no verb form of the word as there is for 'government'. Members of the government can govern, but what is it that members of a network of governance are doing? In reality, the concept tends to capture all forms of collective social coordination outside pure market relations or the family. The problem is that such a broad understanding of governance makes it difficult to distinguish it from all other forms of social coordination. To paraphrase what Aaron Wildavsky (1973) said about another once-popular concept (yes, many years ago), 'If planning is everything, maybe it's nothing.'

In this policy approach to governance there is now a widespread discussion of entities such as 'global governance', 'corporate governance', 'interactive governance' and 'network governance', just to name a few. Our impression is that governance in this public administration and public policy approach should be seen as a meta-concept for all possible forms of order (or disorder) in a number of different settings – from the very local to the global and from the very political and state centred to various private networks that exist outside and have a minimal relation to the state. It may be possible to assess the quality of governance in specific sectors with this approach (see Levi-Faur 2012). However, it goes without saying that 'assessing the quality of governance' as it is understood in this policy approach for a whole country, region or even a city cannot be accomplished in any meaningful way. Leading scholars in this approach also argue that it is not a feasible enterprise to try to establish quantifiable measures of this type of governance for comparing analyses. Instead, they argue for qualitative 'process-tracing' case studies (Torfing et al. 2012, p. 84). While we think that this policy approach to governance empirically captures an important development in Western liberal democracies, the conceptual net is simply far too big for assessing what goes on in a country as a whole. A second problem is that there are very few normative analyses of what should constitute 'good' or 'high quality' in this approach to governance because it is usually unrelated to the type of measures of human well-being discussed earlier. Thirdly, this approach to governance is almost completely detached from the problems of administrative capacity in developing or transition countries. What can be done within this approach is to assess governance in particular sectors, such as the healthcare system, in a country or region or at certain levels of government, such as the city or village level in 'Denmark-type' countries.

### Participatory (Democratic) Governance

A second approach to 'governance' is what has become known as 'participatory governance'. This approach emphasizes the role that ordinary citizens can play in influencing politics outside (or beside) the traditional channels in representative democracy, such as voting and activity in political parties. A strong focus in this approach is given to various forms of deliberative practices in which citizens can discuss and form opinions about how to solve various collective problems (Bellina et al. 2009; Bevir 2010). This is inspired by theories emphasizing the importance of broad-based and open systems for collective deliberation in public decision making either as a complement or as an alternative to the system of representative democracy. Another important part of this approach is how various 'grass roots' organizations can become involved and consulted in policymaking as well as in taking responsibility for the provision of public services. The development of this approach can be seen as a response to what has become known as the 'democratic deficit' problem in many international organizations, the paramount example being the European Union. It is, however, also applied at the very local level when citizens are given a potential 'voice' outside the electoral-parliamentary system, such as in public hearings and other organized deliberative processes (Bevir 2010; Popovski and Cheema 2010).

The discussion about the advantages of new and more participatory methods for engaging citizens in public decision making in liberal democracies and the effects of increased possibilities for deliberation is in itself interesting. In our view, the problem of an increasing 'democratic deficit' is in many cases real. There are, however, two main problems with 'democratic governance' from the perspective of increasing the relevance of political science by focusing on the part of the political system that turns out to have a significant effect on people's life situations. One is that democratic governance blurs the distinction between 'access to power' and 'exercise of power'. As argued by Fukuyama (2014), this concept is built on the so far unrealized hope that there is no conflict between simultaneously realizing representative democracy and state capacity. The second is that so far the lack of conceptual precision in this approach has prevented the production of any standard measure for this concept that can be used in comparative research.

## Good Governance

What is interesting is that at the same time as the aforementioned approaches to governance started to mushroom, a very different idea of what this concept entails saw the light of day. The background of this approach was not located in studies of public administration and public policy in mature Western democracies but instead in discussions in research about development and (the lack of) economic growth in Third-World (and later transition) countries. In common parlance, the approach argued that the institutionalized 'rules of the game' should have a more central role in social science research, especially for explaining variation in social and economic development (Greif 2005; North 1990; Shirley 2005; Smith 2007). In this approach, which we prefer to call the 'political economy approach to governance', the importance of informal institutions has often been stressed by leading scholars (North 1998; Ostrom 1990). However, in empirical research, these 'rules of the game' have de facto become oriented towards state-centred variables. These are, for example, states' administrative capacity, the degree to which the rule-of-law principles are respected, the level of corruption in the public sector, the effectiveness and professionalism in the public administration, the secure enforcement of property rights and meritocratic recruitment of civil servants (Smith 2007). An early important empirical result was produced by Evans and Rauch (1999), who showed that a Weberian type of public administration had a positive impact on economic growth for developing countries.

'Good governance' is now used, in particular, by many national development agencies and international organizations, such as the World Bank and the United Nations. One example is the International Monetary Fund, which in 1996 declared that 'promoting good governance in all its aspects, including by ensuring the rule of law, improving the efficiency and accountability of the public sector, and tackling corruption, as essential elements of a framework within which economies can prosper' (Rothstein 2012, p. 143). In development policy circles, this 'good governance' agenda has to a large extent replaced what was known as the 'Washington consensus'. This approach stated that economic growth could be created by systematic deregulations of markets, tightening of public spending, guarantees for property rights and large-scale privatizations (Serra and Stiglitz 2008). The reason why this strategy did not work was, according to many observers, that poor countries lacked the necessary types of institutions that were 'taken for granted' in neoclassical economics (Rodrik 1999).

As should be obvious, what is understood as 'governance' in this development research perspective is very different from the approach that has come out of the post-Weberian critique of the hierarchical model of top-down steering in public administration analysis centred on problems in liberal Western democracies. It is also very different from the 'democratic governance' approach. In the political economy approach to development, governance is a very state-centred concept referring mainly to specific traits in the court system and public administration (Norris 2012). A first conclusion is that many of the complaints that the governance concept is ill defined (Fukuyama 2011, p. 469; Lynn 2012, pp. 49ff) stem from the fact that these three almost completely different approaches use the same term, each with its own specific intellectual as well as policy background. We would argue that much of the conceptual confusion in governance research is caused by the conflation of these three very different approaches to the subject.[1] A second conclusion is that since the development approach has a more restricted idea of where 'governance' is located, the possibility for creating a definition that is specific and precise enough to be operationalized for assessing and measuring governance in a specific country should increase. This is also why, for example, Rothstein and Teorell (2008) argue that the term 'quality of government' (QoG) should be preferred as the opposite of corruption instead of 'good governance'.

If QoG is the opposite of corruption, how should this concept be defined? In what follows we will specify a number of dimensions on which this theoretical enterprise has to make choices. In this we rely heavily of the approach to concept formation (and mis-formation) in political science that goes back to Giovanni Sartori (1970) and that has been expanded by, for example, David Collier, John Gerring (2012) and Andreas Schedler (for a summary of the discussion, see Schedler 2010). It should be kept in mind that we are striving for a definition of QoG that can be operationalized in such a way that we can actually

---

[1]  To this conceptual 'Tower of Babel' we could add approaches such as 'global governance', corporate governance, meta-governance and regulatory governance.

measure the level of QoG in different countries (or regions or cities or branches of public administration within these entities).

## Normative or Empirical Strategy

For an understanding of what should be seen as the opposite of corruption, Heywood and Rose (2015) have made an important point, namely, that we would not be satisfied with just 'no corruption'. The reason is that this is a far too low a threshold for what we ought to demand from those who are entrusted with public office. Our demand is not just that these agents should refrain from corruption but that we as citizens (and taxpayers) are entitled to expect something more than the absence of corruption. This could, of course, just be competence, but we will argue that there should be a more basic normative standard for how people entrusted to provide public services ought to behave. The issue is thus whether QoG should be defined by a certain norm that pertains to how government power is exercised or whether, as argued by Fukuyama (2013), this conceptualization should be confined to more empirical 'things', such as bureaucratic autonomy and capacity.

There are four reasons why we think a normative definition is necessary. Firstly, terms such as 'good' (as in 'good governance') and 'quality' (as in 'quality of government'), not to mention 'corruption', are inherently normative. Something is 'good' or has high/low 'quality' in relation to a certain norm (or norms), and it is therefore necessary to specify this norm. To state that something or someone is corrupt is doubtless a normative judgement. Trying to define 'good' governance while ignoring the normative issue of what should constitute 'good' simply defies logic. Secondly, the empirical results show that when people make up their minds about whether or not they find their governments legitimate, how a state's power is exercised turns out to be more important for them than their rights pertaining to the 'access' side of the political system. Moreover, the procedures at the 'output side', such as the rule of law and the absence of corruption, turn out to be more important for political legitimacy than are 'outcomes' in the form of public services or benefits (Gilley 2006). Since perceptions of political legitimacy are inherently normative, we have to conceptualize this norm(s). It should be noted that the legitimacy of how the access side of a democratic system should be organized is, according to Robert Dahl (1989, 2006), based on a single basic norm, namely, 'political equality', which in practice is equal voting rights and equal right to stand for office. Thus, if the procedures that take place at the 'output side' of the political system are more important for citizens when they make up their minds about whether their government is to be considered legitimate than the procedures at the 'input side', we should be able to find the parallel basic norm for this part of the political system. Obviously, it cannot be 'political equality' because most laws and public policies require that citizens should be treated differently (e.g. pay different taxes or get different benefits, subsidies and services depending on their specific situations and circumstances).

Thirdly, the risk with empirical definitions is that they have a tendency to become equal to the outcome we want, to explain that they in practice become tautological. One example is the definition of 'good institutions' provided by Acemoglu and Robinson (2012). Their well-known argument is that it is institutions of a certain kind that promote economic prosperity. Such institutions, they argue, should be 'inclusive'. With this they mean institutions that 'allow and encourage participation by the great mass of people in economic activities that make best use of their talents and skill and enable them to make the choices they wish'. Such institutions should also 'secure private property, an unbiased system of law, and a provision of services that provides a level playing field in which people can exchange and contract'. Moreover, such institutions 'also must permit the entry of new business and allow people to choose their careers'. The list goes on: the institutions that are needed for economic prosperity should also 'distribute power broadly in society' and ensure that 'political power rests with a broad coalition or plurality of groups' (Acemoglu and Robinson 2012, pp. 73 and 80).

The problem with this definition is that it is very close to what the theory intends to explain. How surprised should we be that a society with such 'inclusive' institutions will create a good and prosperous society and that a society with the opposite type of 'extractive' institutions will be bad and poor? What they are saying is basically that a good society will produce a good (or prosperous) society. The same can be said for definitions of QoG that includes effectiveness. The purpose of this conceptual enterprise is to explain why some states are more effective (in producing human well-being) than others, and if we include effectiveness in the very definition of QoG, we will not be able to explain variation in effectiveness.

The central issue is this: if a society decides to organize its public administration according to a certain norm (or set of norms) that states, for example, who will work in this administration and according to which principle(s) civil servants and professionals will make decisions, will this result in higher organizational capacity and competence? Furthermore, will this make it more likely that the politicians will entrust this administration with a certain degree of autonomy? The empirical answer to this question seems to be in the affirmative. For example, if civil servants are recruited based on the norm of impartiality, which means that factual merits for the job in question are what decides recruitment and promotion, this will lead to higher competence and thus to higher state capacity, which, in turn, is likely to lead to increased levels of human well-being (Charron et al. 2013; Dahlström et al. 2011; Rothstein 2012; Rothstein and Tannenberg 2015). Thus, the procedural principle of impartiality translates in practice into meritocracy, which, *inter alia*, leads to increased competence and capacity in the public sector. The question raised by Fukuyama (2013, p. 349) – that is, whether impartiality as the basic norm for how a state interacts with its citizens will result in increased state capacity – is thus no longer only 'simply asserted' but also empirically grounded. Simply put, there are now a number of reasonably good empirical indicators showing that impartiality as the procedural norm will lead to better outcomes in terms of lower corruption and higher state capacity.

A final reason for a normative definition of QoG instead of pointing at specific empirically existing institutions is that if we look at countries that are judged to have high levels of QoG, their political and legal institutions, as well as their systems of public administration, show remarkable variation. This implies that simply exporting such institutions (or a specific state's institutional configuration) from high QoG to low QoG countries will not work to improve QoG. When this has been tried, the results have not been encouraging (Andrews 2013). The reason seems to be that it is not the specific institutional configuration of the state and the public administration but the basic norm under which the institutions operate that is the crucial factor.

## Should the Definition Be Based on Political Procedures or Policy Substance?

Is QoG something that should be defined by reference to a set of political procedures, or should it be defined by reference to certain policies or outcomes. An example of the latter is the well-known definition of 'good governance' provided by Daniel Kaufmann and colleagues at the World Bank, which, among other things, includes 'sound policies' (Kaufmann et al. 2004). Political philosophers, however, have argued for including the 'moral content' of the enacted laws or policies into the definition (Agnafors 2013). The well-known problem with any substantive definition of democracy, and thereby QoG, is why people, who can be expected to have very different views about policies, should accept them. Since we are opting for a definition that can be universally accepted and applied, including specific policies becomes problematic. To use Rawls' (2005) terminology, political legitimacy requires an 'overlapping consensus' about the basic institutions for justice in a society so that citizens will continue to support them even when they have incommensurable conceptions of 'the meaning, value and purpose of human life' and even if their group would lose political power. This is, of course, less likely to be the case if specific (sound) policies and moral content of the laws are included in the definition of QoG.

Including as the World Bank does 'sound policies' in the definition also raises the quite problematic question of whether international (mostly economic) experts really can be expected to be in possession of reliable answers to the question of what 'sound policies' are. For example, should pensions, healthcare or education be privately or publicly funded (or a mix of these)? To what extent and how should financial institutions be regulated? Secondly, such a definition of QoG that is not restricted to procedures but includes the substance of policies raises what is known as the 'Platonian-Leninist problem'. If those with superior knowledge decide policies, the democratic process will be emptied of most substantial issues. The argument against the Platonian-Leninist alternative to democracy has been put forward by one of the leading democratic theorists, Robert Dahl, in the following way: '[I]ts extraordinary demands on the knowledge and virtue of the guardians are all but impossible to satisfy in practice' (Dahl 1989, p. 65).

All this implies that a strictly procedural definition of QoG is to be preferred. This also follows from the desire to strive for a definition of

QoG that is parallel to how the 'access side' of liberal representative democracy usually is defined, which speaks for a strictly procedural definition. The system known as 'liberal representative democracy' should not in itself favour any specific set of policies or moral standards (except those that are connected to the democratic procedures as such). From the perspective of legitimacy, it should be noted that there is ample evidence from experimental studies showing that when people decide whether a decision by a public authority that affects them is just, they do not only take into consideration the 'what did I get' issue. Instead, 'how they got it' – the fairness in the actual procedure in which the decision was implemented – is in most cases more important for them to accept the outcome, especially in cases where the outcome is a negative one (Levi et al. 2009; Tyler 1992).

There is a well-known drawback to all procedural definitions of political processes for decision making, namely, that they cannot offer a guarantee against morally bad decisions. As is well known, there is no guarantee against perfectly democratically made decisions in a representative democracy resulting in severe violations of the rights of minorities and individuals. As Mann (2005) has argued, there is a 'dark side' to democracy. This is also the case for any procedural definition of QoG, be it ethical universalism (Mungiu-Pippidi 2006), impersonal rule (North et al. 2009), bureaucratic autonomy and capacity (Fukuyama 2013) or impartiality in the exercise of public power (Rothstein and Teorell 2008). In this approach, we think that the strategy suggested by John Rawls (1971) is the right one. His central idea is that if a society structures its systems for making and enforcing collective decisions in a fair way, this will increase the *likelihood* that the outcomes are normatively just. As Rawls stated: '[S]ubstantive and formal justice tend to go together and therefore ... at least grossly unjust institutions are never, or at any rate rarely, impartial and consistently administered' (Rawls 1971, p. 59).

## The Opposite of Corruption: Quality of Government as Impartiality

A state regulates relations to its citizens along two dimensions. One is the 'input side', which relates to *access* to public authority. This is where we in democracies find rules about elections, party financing, the right to stand for office and the formation of cabinets. The other side of the political system is the 'output side', which refers to the way in which that political authority is *exercised*. On the input side, where the access to power and thereby the content of policies are determined, as stated earlier, the most widely accepted basic regulatory principle has been formulated by Dahl (1989) as that of 'political equality'. This is also Rawls' (2005) basic idea on how to construct a non-utilitarian society based on his well-known principles of justice. Political equality certainly implies impartial treatment on the input side of the system, and this makes political equality and impartiality partially overlapping concepts (Rawls 2005; cf. Goodin 2004, p. 97). Elections have to be administered by the existing government, but if they are to be considered free and, in particular, *fair*, the ruling party must refrain from organizing them in a manner that undermines the opposition's potential to obtain power. That is, in order to be seen as legitimate, free and fair elections must be administered by impartial government institutions (Choe 1997; Norris 2014; Schedler 2002, p. 44). But again, the impartial organization of elections does not imply that the content or outcome of the process is impartial. On the contrary, the reason that many, if not most, people are active in politics is that they are motivated by very partisan interests. A working democracy therefore must be able to implement the partisan interests produced by the input side of the system in an impartial way. The question is how this can be conceptualized. Based on Strömberg (2000), Rothstein and Teorell (2008) have suggested the following: *when implementing laws and policies, government officials shall not take anything into consideration about the citizen/case that is not beforehand stipulated in the policy or the law*. In this context, impartiality is not a demand on actors on the input side of the political system but first and foremost an attribute of the actions taken by civil servants, professional corpses in public service, law enforcement personnel and the like. In order to effectuate this ideal, it may also be necessary, however, to inscribe impartiality as an ideal into the mind-sets of these actors.

To see why this definition of QoG is universal, it is useful to compare it to Dahl's idea of 'political equality' as a basic norm for democracy. Every particular democratic state is, in its institutional configuration, different. It should suffice to point at the extreme variation in the electoral systems in, for example, the Swiss, Danish and British democracies. There are in fact innumerable ways to organize a national democracy (presidentialism versus parliamentarism, unicameralism versus bicameralism, proportional versus majoritarian electoral systems, variation in the power of the courts, federalism versus unitarianism, the role of referendums, the strength of local governments, and so on). As long as the principle of equality in access to power is not violated (e.g. by giving one specific political party the right to rule or by refusing to give some specific group of citizens the right to stand for office or take part in the public debate), we call such differing political systems, as in Finland and the United States, 'democracies'. The reason is that all institutional arrangements on the input side in a representative democracy should be possible to justify from the viewpoint of 'political equality'.

Impartiality as the parallel legitimatizing and defining principle for the output side can in a similar way also encompass various administrative practices. As shown by Andrews (2013), the specific administrative and organizational configurations of governments deemed to be of high quality are in effect quite different. QoG as impartiality is, of course, in line with the idea of a procedural definition, which means that it can encompass very different policies and does not rule out support for specific groups or interests.

Kurer (2005, p. 230) has also tried to define corruption in terms of impartiality. His definition is that 'corruption involves a holder of public office violating the impartiality principle in order to achieve private gain.' As Kurer argues, the advantage with this definition of corruption is that what counts as a breach of impartiality is fairly universally understood and thus not related to how such things as 'abuse' or 'misuse' of public power are viewed in different cultures. The advantage of this definition is that impartiality rules out not only all forms of corruption but also practices such as clientelism, patronage, nepotism, political favouritism, discrimination and other forms of 'particularism'.

One way to think about the logic of impartiality is to make an analogy to sports, for example, soccer (football). The football clubs in a national (or regional or local) football league are in stark competition, and they all really want to win the league, almost at all costs. However, the football clubs also want to secure the existence of a functioning and well-organized league that has legitimacy both among their own supporters and among supporters in general. If this is going to work, the clubs will have to come together and produce two things. One is a set of rules for the games that all 'reasonable' clubs are willing to accept. They also need a set of rules for organization of the league (how transfers of players should be done, how to handle teams whose supporters interfere with the matches and so on). For this to work, they need to produce officials (referees and league managers) who are guided by the principle of impartiality. For example, individuals who are 'die hard' fans of a specific club in the league will not be accepted as referees. A referees who is willing to favour a team for money will be seen as corrupt and will be shunned by supporters of all teams. If club A knows that club B has bribed the referee, it will either leave the match or start overbidding in bribes, and then the league will collapse (as was the case in the famous 2006 football corruption case in the Italian National League) (cf. Hill 2008). Also, players usually do not like to play on a team where they can take for granted that some of their team-mates are 'on the take' (this is apparently why so many players from South America prefer to play in Europe). It should be noted that the importance of impartiality in the governing a football leagues seems to be universally understood and accepted. The Confederations of African and the South American Football do not differ in this respect from their European and North American counterparts. Clubs and supporters from these parts of the world do not think of the rulebook produced by the Fédération Internationale de Football Association (FIFA) as a Western imperialist post-colonial treaty alien to their cultures. After all, we are talking about the world's most popular sport.

As stated earlier, some have argued that it is necessary to take the 'substance' of policies and laws into account when defining what should count as QoG. Here the important point is that the referees (or league managers) do not decide any rulings or make any official judgements about the substance of how well the team plays. In this respect, 'the input' (i.e. how teams are playing and what system of defence they use) is not in the domain of the 'public officials' who are responsible for organization of the league. The referees also do not have anything to say about whether the teams play 'beautiful football'. A team does not get extra points for playing well. Thus, if the input in the match is 'good' or 'bad', to use Agnafors (2013) terms, 'the morality of the laws' is outside the domain of what the public officials are to decide. A team that plays really badly, what in Swedish is known as 'pig football',[2] but

---

[2]  This is when a team, after having scored the first goal, goes for an extreme defensive strategy, trying only to destroy any organized play by the other team.

that makes more goals than the opposing team will still be the winner. Using the terminology from the World Bank, the officials in this example do not make decisions about which tactics or strategy on the field is to be counted as 'sound football'. However, note that a league with good, impartial referees (and league managers) is likely to play much better and more fair football than a league that lacks this 'QoG', but, of course, there can be no guarantee. We simply have to hope that Rawls was right when he stated that there is a causal connection from procedural justice to substantive justice (Rawls 1971, p. 59).

Rawls also stated that 'it is supposed that if institutions are reasonably just, then it is of great importance that the authorities should be impartial and not influenced by personal, monetary, or other irrelevant considerations in their handling of particular cases' (Rawls 1971, p. 58). One should note here that the demand for 'reasonableness' pertains only to when the clubs decide about the rules (institutions) for the league and the rules for the matches, not for how the different teams should be playing (i.e. the input side). The clubs do not come together and reason about whether they all should use the 4-4-2 system or some other setup when they play. In politics, this is equivalent to a situation in which the opposing political parties can hopefully come together and try to be reasonable when deciding about a state's constitutional and administrative arrangements, but not about their specific programmes. Thus, this is where Rawls' famous 'overlapping consensus' can occur (cf. Rothstein and Teorell 2008).

In the political philosophy discussion about impartiality, this distinction between which norms should guide the content versus procedural sides of the political system is readily seen in Brian Barry's important book, *Justice as Impartiality*. Barry argues that impartiality should be a normative criterion in the exercise of political power: 'like cases should be treated alike' (Barry 1995, p. 126). His idea of 'second-order impartiality' implies that the input side of the political system should be arranged so that it gives no special favour to any conception of 'the good'. However, as Barry readily admits, his theory 'accepts that a demand of neutrality cannot be imposed on the outcomes' (Barry 1995, p. 238). Accordingly, when it comes to decisions about the content of the policies that governments should pursue, it is not neutrality or impartiality but 'reasonableness' that is his main criterion (Barry 1995, p. 238). By this he means that people engaged in the political process should give sound arguments based on a secular understanding of knowledge for why they prefer certain policies over others. In Barry's words, 'What is required is as far as possible a polity in which arguments are weighed and the best arguments win, rather than one in which all that can be said is that votes are counted and the side with the most votes wins' (Barry 1995, p. 103).

The implication is the one argued for here, namely, that impartiality cannot be a moral basis for the content of policies that individuals, interest groups and political parties pursue on the input side of the political system because reasonableness is not the same as impartiality. For example, in a given situation, there may be good reasons for lowering pensions and increasing support to families with children. This is, however, not the same as being impartial between these two groups because there is no such thing as an impartial way to decide in a case such as this.

What is presented here is thus not of the grand ambition that Barry, Rawls and other political philosophers have pursued, namely, to construct a universal theory of social and political justice. The ambition is more modest, namely, to construct a theory of what should count as the opposite of corruption, that is, as QoG. The implication is that when a policy has been decided upon by the representative democratic system, be it deemed just or unjust according to whatever universal theory of justice one would apply, QoG implies that it has to be implemented in accordance with the principle of impartiality.

Those who want to include policy substance in the definition of QoG would in this sports analogy be thinking more like what occurs for referees in a beauty contest or maybe also in figure skating. Here the referees not only follow and implement a set of rules about how the contenders are supposed to appear, such as how long they should perform and what acts are acceptable. Instead, the referees also make decisions about how beautiful the contenders look or, in the case of figure skating, the artistic component of the performance. Thus, in contrast to the referees in football, the referees in beauty contests and figure skating also decide about what is good at the input of the performance. Here impartiality is, we dare to say, neither desirable nor possible.

The conclusion we draw from this thought experiment is that the probability that a political system that builds access to power on the fair principle of 'political equality' will produce outcomes that increase social and political justice is higher than if access to power is organized in a different manner. The equivalent for the administrative side of the state would then be that if implementation of policies is based on a norm such as impartiality, the *probability* for normatively good outcomes would increase. As argued earlier, empirical research shows that the latter case is more probable than the former; that is, high QoG has a much stronger impact on measures of human well-being than representative democracy has. Given a fair political order such as high QoG, this is what we can expect but, again, not guarantee. This is what Philippe Van Parijs (2011) has labelled the 'Rawls-Machiavelli programme', which, he argues, has two components: from Rawls he takes what one should regard as a just political order and from Machiavelli what we, from empirical knowledge, can suppose is feasible for 'real people' to accomplish (Van Parijs 2011).

An argument against defining QoG as based on the principle of impartiality in the exercise of public power is that, in theory, a Nazi extermination camp could be administered in an impartial way (Agnafors 2013; Fukuyama 2013). The first thing to be said about comments such as this is that an overwhelming part of the historical research about how the Third Reich was administrated gives a completely different picture. Instead of impartiality, the modus operandi of the Nazi state was systematic politically and ideologically motivated favouritism, personalistic rule, clientelism, disregard and manipulation of rule-of-law principles, disregarding professional knowledge and ad-hoc decision making (Aly 2007; Broszat 1981; Evans 2009). The idea of the impartially administrated Nazi state or concentration camp belongs to the 'crazy cases' approach in political philosophy, which, according to Goodin (1982), strongly increases the discipline's irrelevance. As he stated:

First we are invited to reflect on a few hypothetical examples – the more preposterous, the better apparently. Then, with very little further argument or analysis, general moral principles are quickly inferred from our intuitive responses to these 'crazy cases' ... Whatever their role in settling deeper philosophical issues, bizarre hypotheticals are of little help in resolving real dilemmas of public policy. (Goodin 1982, p. 8)

Secondly, the same problem exists for the procedural principles following from political equality that forms the basic norm for representative democracy – there is nothing in this norm that hinders the majority in an ever so correct procedural representative democracy to decide illiberal policies that seriously violate human rights for individuals or minorities (King 1999; Zakaria 2003). This problem of possible normatively unwanted outcomes is unavoidable if we want to stay within a procedural definition of QoG (or liberal democracy). This is why most democratization activists and organizations nowadays usually speak of 'democracy and human rights' as if they are inseparable. There is certainly nothing that hinders policy activists and policy organizations to start promoting 'QoG and human rights' (something that we certainly would support following our earlier discussion of the connection between human rights and anti-corruption discourses). However, from a theoretical perspective, democracy, corruption and QoG are separate things and should not be conflated because we want to know how they are empirically related. As stated by Fukuyama (2013, p. 351), we probably would not like to 'argue that the U.S. military is a low-quality one because it does things we disapprove of, say, invading Iraq?' If we define QoG by 'good outcomes' or include the 'moral status of the laws' and/or the 'public ethos' (Agnafors 2013), we will be creating a conceptual tautology saying that a society with a high moral standard and a good 'public ethos' will result in good outcomes. This is like saying that the good society is a cause for achieving the good society. Simply put, we must have the intellectual courage to admit that a public organization can have high quality and low corruption in doing what it does even if from a moral perspective we disapprove of the policies it is carrying out. It goes without saying that we as individuals can often think that a public policy is grossly unfair and unjust even if it is decided by a perfectly correct democratic procedure. As we see it, this is just one side of how majoritarian democracy is supposed to work. After all, most people become engaged in politics because they are partisan to some cause, group or idea. However, the point we want to make is that the 'opposite of corruption' implies that we should normatively prefer even policies that we disagree with to be implemented in an impartial way. If we include the substance of policies in the definition, QoG is just simply when a public authority efficiently implements the policies that we happen to like. Moreover, a reasonably high level of QoG can be seen as a prerequisite for establishing democracy (Fukuyama 2014). Almost all stable 'elite' democracies in Northwestern Europe first managed to create state capacity and get corruption under control – and then they became democracies.

The advantage of a procedural strategy is that it is more likely to attain a broad-based acceptance (i.e. Rawls' 'overlapping consensus') even in a society with groups that have incommensurable ideas of 'the good'. If QoG would include 'the moral status of the laws' (Agnafors 2013), as defined by some ideology, it is very unlikely that a Rawlsian 'overlapping consensus' can be reached. However, if we decided to stay within a procedural definition of QoG, as the empirical results mentioned earlier show, this will increase the probability of outcomes that increase human well-being in the form of extended capabilities for citizens, as suggested by Amartya Sen's theory of justice. Empirically, as argued earlier, there is ample evidence that this is also the case (Charron et al. 2013; Holmberg and Rothstein 2012; Teorell 2009). In sum, the procedural strategy in defining QoG can be said to rest on an assumed probability that if the political system of a society is based on procedures that can be normatively motived as fair, this will increase the likelihood of normatively just outcomes. The alternative substantive definitional strategy is less likely to achieve 'overlapping consensus' because there is not much agreement in many countries of the world on what should constitute what economists argue are 'sound policies' or the philosophers claim to be the right 'moral status of the laws'.

## Should the Definition of QoG Be Multi- or Unidimensional?

Several attempts to define QoG have argued for a multidimensional or 'complex' strategy. QoG should entail that decisions in the public administration adhere to 'efficiency', 'public ethos', 'good decision making', 'transparency', accountability' and 'stability', to name a few. Others have argued for a unidimensional strategy (Mungiu-Pippidi 2006; Rothstein and Teorell 2008). There are several drawbacks with the multidimensional strategy (also sometimes labelled 'thick' conceptualizations). The first is that we may treat what is basically an empirical question by definitional fiat. Simply put, we want to explain why high QoG makes some states' public administration more efficient than others, and this implies that we cannot include efficiency in the definition of QoG because we do not want to state that efficiency explains efficiency. The same goes for 'good decision making' (as suggested by Agnafors 2013) and 'capacity' (as suggested by Fukuyama 2013). We want a definition of QoG that can be helpful in explaining why the public administration in some states has a better capacity for making good decisions than the public administration in other states (or regions or cities), and if we include what we want to explain in the definition, this explanatory purpose becomes impossible.

The problem with defining the opposite of corruption as 'account-ability' is that this term refers only a process or a tool. No organization or bureaucrat can be held accountable in general because you are always held accountable according to some specified normative standard(s). Heywood and Rose (2015, p. 112) point at 'integrity', which they define as 'doing the right thing' and also doing it 'in the right way', but they do not provide a clear definition of what should be this 'right thing' or 'right way'. They state that 'where integrity is upheld, actions taken are consistent with the "proper" means of act-ing.' However, in a thoroughly corrupt country, the 'proper' means of acting for a high-level civil servant may, for example, be nepotism when recruiting personnel. Thus, without defining the normative standard(s) for when we can say that corruption occurs, accountability as well as transparency and integrity may be important instruments (or tools), but they lack conceptual substance.

A well-known problem with multidimensional definitions is how to handle a situation when a state for which we want to measure QoG shows very different values on the dimensions. World Bank researchers include five different dimensions, and Agnafors (2013), for example, includes no fewer than six dimensions. The question then becomes how to handle a situation where the rule of law is zero but where there is maximum efficiency (or stability, or public ethos, or good decision making). Would this be a state with 50 per cent QoG? As Agnafors (2013) readily admits, there can be 'no universal and complete weigh-ing procedure' for solving this problem. His solution is that 'one can perform an *incomplete* weighing, at least in theory, because it will be inescapably messy in practice.'

This line of reasoning is a luxury that many political philosophers think they can afford because they seldom engage in empirical research or take responsibility for the administrative or practical side of their policy suggestions (Wolff 2011). As Agnafors (2013) stated, he does not want to take responsibility for how his many criteria for what should be included in QoG should be weighed when they come into conflict. He readily admits that his method is 'incomplete', and then he adds that he does not want to address 'the extent to which such incompleteness can be overcome'. Avoiding responsibility in this way does not work for political scientists who care about the relevance of their research for peoples' well-being. Producing a definition that is so thick that it cannot be operationalized in any meaningful sense will not help us to answer the question of why some states are much more successful than others in implementing policies that cater to the basic needs (capabilities) of their citizens. If we were to follow this conceptual strategy, the question of what politics can do against, for example, severe child deprivation or extremely high rates of women dying during childbirth, will never be answered. Here Agnafors (2013) and many other contemporary political philosophers stand in sharp contradiction to Rawls, who argued that 'political philosophy must describe workable political arrangements that can gain support from real people' (from Wenar 2012). Rawls' famous theory of justice does entail two basic principles but, *nota bene*, they are lexically ordered, making it is clear which of them that has priority (Wenar 2012).

As argued by Van Parijs (2011, p.1), '[I]t is sound intellectual policy ... not to make our concepts too fat.' He continues, and we agree, '[F]at concepts hinder clear thinking and foster wishful thinking. By packing many good things under a single label, one is easily misled into believing that they never clash.' As known ever since William Ockham's days, ontological parsimony is an analytical virtue. In sum, the conceptual obesity that is suggested by Agnafors (2013) and many others for what should constitute QoG will inevitably lead to explanatory impotence and thereby become unusable for policy recommendations. This is not only a question of internal academic civilities and intellectual hair splitting because we now know that low QoG has severe effects on human well-being.

## Impartiality and the Rule of Law

This is also the reason why the impartiality principle cannot be equated to the rule-of-law principle. While impartiality is a central ingredient in most definitions of the rule of law (Versteeg and Ginsburg 2016), the former also includes the aforementioned professional groups that implement public policies but for which the modus operandi of the rule of law is not applicable (Rothstein and Teorell 2008). An analysis of four different comparative measures[3] of the extent to which rule-of-law principles are respected and implemented in different countries finds some very interesting results (Versteeg and Ginsburg 2016). Although the four indexes are built on quite different conceptual strategies, empirically, they correlate on a surprisingly high level. The pair-wise correlation between three of them exceeds .95 (the fourth is ~.80), and they also correlate at this high level with the measure of corruption constructed by Transparency International (Versteeg and Ginsburg 2016) and with the measure of 'impartial administration' constructed at the Quality of Government Institute (Dahlberg et al. 2013). From this the authors conclude that the reason why the differently constructed indexes of the rule of law correlate so highly is that they seem to 'fit into a broader umbrella concept of impartiality' which they think might be 'a higher order concept' that connects corruption and the rule of law, thereby capturing the 'essence' of both indicators. The authors also argue that although impartiality is a 'thin' concept, relating only to procedures and excluding the normative substance of the rules, the 'thicker' conceptualization of the rule of law does not add anything. In other words, the 'thicker' conceptualizations of the rule of law that includes the normative substance of the rules 'do not matter'. One conclusion from this is that we here may have found empirical support for Rawls' (1971) presumption that 'thin' procedural justice is likely to result in 'thick' substantive justice.

## Quality of Government as the Opposite of Corruption

The conclusion is thus that we should strive for a normative, procedural, universal and parsimonious definition of what should count as the opposite of corruption (QoG) that, moreover, can be operationalized and measured. The definition should not include the system of access to power (e.g. representative democracy) because we want to be able to explain the relation between representative democracy and QoG. It also should not include things such as efficiency or capacity because we want to be able to explain whether QoG has a positive or negative impact on these things. Following the Rawls-Machiavelli programme as suggested by Van Parijs, this conceptual strategy can

---

[3] The indexes are constructed by the Heritage Foundation, Freedom House, the World Bank and the World Justice Project.

be seen as resting on the assumption (or hope) that if we as political scientists can suggest 'just institutions' for making and implementing collectively binding decisions, the people who come to operate these 'just institutions' are also likely to produce morally good outcomes. The alternative, that we should suggest specific ('sound') policies or prescribe the 'moral status' of the laws, runs in the face of the need to reach an 'overlapping consensus' for how collectively binding decisions should be made and implemented. Again, no such procedural definition (of democracy or QoG) can work as a guarantee against morally bad outcomes – we are dealing with probabilities, not absolute certainty. Since empirical research shows that higher levels of QoG (but not representative democracy) are related to higher levels of human well-being (and political legitimacy), following Sen's capability-oriented theory of justice, we as political scientists have a moral obligation to increase our ambitions to define, measure and study what takes place at the 'output side' of the political system. This is not an internal academic affair in which you can sacrifice what actually works for what would be an ideal (but un-implementable) definition. We have no doubt in stating that a major part of human misery in today's world is caused by the fact that a majority of the world's population is forced to live under dysfunctional (low-quality) government institutions.

The impartiality definition suggested by Rothstein and Teorell (2008) that we have developed here is normative, fairly precise, unidimensional and, as argued earlier, can be applied universally. As opposed to empty definitions such as 'the misuse of public power for private gain' (Karklins 2005) or 'the interest of the public' (Philp 2015), where what should count as 'misuse' or the 'public interest' remain unspecified, the definition we propose clearly specifies which norm is transgressed when corruption occurs. The definition we propose is admittedly 'thin', but it should be recalled that we have been trying to find the basic norm that can serve as the core for what is to be understood as corruption and the opposite of corruption.

As has been shown in other studies from the Quality of Government Institute, this definition of QoG can be operationalized and measured in both expert surveys and surveys with representative samples of the population (Charron et al. 2013; Dahlström et al. 2011). Neither experts nor ordinary people seem to have problems understanding and answering the battery of survey questions that follows from this definition of QoG. Moreover, these measures largely perform in the expected way when correlated with various outcome measures, such as measures of human well-being. In closing, we argue that the opposite of corruption can be defined, measured and operationalized. This implies that we can find explanations for the huge variation in QoG that exists between societies over time and in space. Some of these explanations may be situated in historical and structural factors that are beyond our capacity to change, whereas others may be within the reach of effective policies (Rothstein and Teorell 2015). While changing corruption in policies and institutions may well be a Herculean task, especially if the collective action theory we have put forward is correct, a number historical cases show that this can be done (Mungiu-Pippidi 2015; Rothstein and Uslaner 2016).

# References

Acemoglu, Daron and James A. Robinson. 2008. 'Persistence of Power, Elites, and Institutions'. *American Economic Review* 98(1): 267–93.

and James A. Robinson. 2012. *Why Nations Fail: The Origins of Power, Prosperity and Poverty*. London: Profile.

Afrobarometer: Round III 2005–2006 [merged eighteen-country data set]. Cape Town, South Africa: Institute for Democracy in South Africa, DataFirst.

Agnafors, Marcus. 2013. 'Quality of Government: Towards a More Complex Definition'. *American Political Science Review* 107(3): 433–55.

Ahlers, Anna L. 2014. *Rural Policy Implementation in Contemporary China*. London: Routledge.

and Gunter Schubert. 2011. '"Adaptive Authoritarianism" in Contemporary China: Identifying Zones of Legitimacy Building'. In *Reviving Legitimacy: Lessons for and from China*, eds. D. Zhenglai and S. Guo. Lanham, MD: Lexington Books.

Alatas, S. Hussein. 1968. *The Sociology of Corruption: The Nature, Function, Causes and Prevention of Corruption*. Singapore: D. Moore Press.

1977. *Intellectuals in Developing Societies*. London: Cass.

1999. *Corruption and the Destiny of Asia*. Englewood Cliffs, NJ: Prentice-Hall.

Aly, Götz. 2007. *Hitler's Beneficiaries: Plunder, Race War, and the Nazi Welfare State*. New York: Metropolitan.

Andrews, Matt. 2013. *The Limits of Institutional Reform in Development: Changing Rules for Realistic Solutions*. Cambridge University Press.

Andvig, Jens Chr., Odd-Helge Fjeldstad, Inge Amundsen, Tone Sissener and Tina Søreide. 2001. *Corruption: A Review of Contemporary Research*. Bergen, Norway: Chr. Michelsen Institute.

Aristotle. 2000. *Politics*, ed. B. Jowett. Mineola, NY: Dover Publications.

Arneson, Richard. 1998. 'The Priority of the Right over the Good Rides Again'. In *Impartiality, Neutrality and Justice*, ed. P. Kelly. Edinburgh University Press.

Arriola, Leonardo R. 2009. 'Patronage and Political Stability in Africa'. *Comparative Political Studies* 42(10): 1339–62.

Ashkanasy, Neal M., Celeste Wilderom and Mark F. Peterson. 2011. *The Handbook of Organizational Culture and Climate*, 2nd edn. Thousand Oaks, CA: Sage.

Bacio-Terracino, Julio. 2008. 'Corruption as a Violation of Human Rights', International Council on Human Rights Policy, available at http://pap ers.ssrn.com/sol3/papers.cfm?abstract_id=1107918.

Balla, Balint. 1972. *Kaderverwaltung*. Stuttgart: Soziologische Gegenwartsfragen.

Banfield, Edward R. 1958. *The Moral Basis of a Backward Society*. New York: Free Press.

Barry, Brian. 1995. *Justice as Impartiality*. New York: Clarendon Press.

Bates, Robert H. 2008. *When Things Fell Apart: State Failure in Late Century Africa*. New York: Cambridge University Press.

Bauhr, Monika. 2012. 'Need or Greed Corruption'. In *Good Government: The Relevance of Political Science*, eds. S. Holmberg and B. Rothstein. Cheltenham: Edward Elgar.

Bell, Daniel A. 2015. *The China Model: Political Meritocracy and the Limits of Democracy*. Princeton, NJ: Princeton University Press.

Bellina, Séverine, Hervé Magro and Violaine de Villemeur. 2009. *Democratic Governance: A New Paradigm for Development?* London: Hurst.

Besley, Timothy. 2007. *Principled Agents? The Political Economy of Good Government*. Oxford University Press.

Bevir, Mark. 2010. *Democratic Governance*. Princeton, NJ: Princeton University Press.

Bicchieri, Chistina and Erte Xiao. 2009. 'Do the Right Thing: But Only If Others Do So'. *Journal of Behavioral Decision Making* 22(2): 191–208.

Birney, Mayling. 2013. 'Decentralization and Veiled Corruption under China's "Rule of Mandates"'. *World Development* 53: 55–67.

Booth, David and Diana Cammack. 2013. *Governance for Development in Africa: Solving Collective Action Problems*. London: Zed Books.

Bracking, Sarah. 2007. *Corruption and Development: The Anti-Corruption Campaigns*. New York: Palgrave Macmillan.

Brante, Thomas. 2014. *Den professionella logiken. Hur vetenskap och praktik förenas i det moderna kunskapssamhället*. Johanneshov, Sweden: MTM.

Bratsis, Peter. 2003. 'The Construction of Corruption, or Rules of Separation and Illusions of Purity in Bourgeois Societies'. *Social Text* 21(4): 9–33.

Bratton, Michael and Nicolas Van de Walle. 1994. 'Neopatrimonial Regimes and Political Transitions in Africa'. *World Politics* 46(4): 453–89.

Brinkerhoff, Derick W. and Arthur A. Goldsmith. 2002. 'Clientelism, Patrimonialism and Democratic Governance: An Overview and Framework for Assessment and Programming', Abt Associates, Bethesda, MD, prepared for USAID, available at http://pdf.usaid.gov/ pdf_docs/Pnacr426.pdf.

Broszat, Martin. 1981. *The Hitler State: The Foundation and Development of the Internal Structure of the Third Reich*. London: Longman.

Bukovansky, Mlada. 2006. 'The Hollowness of Anti-Corruption Discourse'. *Review of International Political Economy* 13(2): 181–209.

Burke, Peter J. and Jan E. Stets. 2009. *Identity Theory*. New York: Oxford University Press.

Burns, John P. 2007. 'Civil Service Reform in China'. *OECD Journal on Budgeting* 7(1): 1–25.

and Zhou Zhiren. 2010. 'Performance Management in the Government of the People's Republic of China: Accountability and Control in the Implementation of Public Policy'. *OECD Journal on Budgeting* 10: 1–28.

Caciagli, Mario. 2006. 'The Long Life of Clientelism in Southern Italy'. In *Comparing Political Corruption and Clientelism*, ed. J. Kawata. Aldershot: Ashgate.

Carmona, Magdalena S. 2009. 'The Obligations of "International Assistance and Cooperation" under the International Covenant on Economic, Social and Cultural Rights. A Possible Entry Point to a Human Rights Based Approach to Millennium Development Goal 8'. *International Journal of Human Rights* 13(1): 86–109.

Çelebi, Kâtip. 1957. *The Balance of Truth*, trans. G. L. Lewis. London: Allen & Unwin.

Charron, Nicholas and Victor Lapuente. 2011. 'Which Dictators Produce Quality of Government?' *Studies in Comparative International Development* 46(4): 397–423.

Victor Lapuente and Bo Rothstein. 2013. *Quality of Government and Corruption from a European Perspective: A Comparative Study of Good Government in EU Regions*. Cheltenham: Edward Elgar.

Chayes, Sarah. 2015. *Thieves of State: Why Corruption Threatens Global Security*. New York: W. W. Norton.

Chen, Xin. 2005. 'The Reform Discourse and China's War on Corruption'. In *Corruption and Good Governance in Asia*, ed. N. Tarling. New York: Routledge.

Choe, Yonhyok. 1997. 'How to Manage Free and Fair Elections: A Comparison of Korea, Sweden and the United Kingdom'. PhD dissertation, Department of Political Science, University of Gothenburg.

Chou, Bill. 2008. 'Does "Good Governance" Matter? Civil Service Reform in China'. *International Journal of Public Administration* 31(1): 54–75.

Cohen, Michael D., James G. March and Johan P. Olsen. 1972. 'A Garbage Can Model of Organizational Choice'. *Administrative Science Quarterly* 17(1): 1–25.

Collins, Paul and Hon S. Chan. 2009. 'State Capacity Building in China: An Introduction'. *Public Administration and Development* 29(1): 1–8.

Cupit, Geoffrey. 2000. 'When Does Justice Require Impartiality?' Political Studies Association UK 50th Annual Conference, London, April 10–13.

Dagger, Richard. 1999. 'The Sandelian Republic and the Encumbered Self'. *Review of Politics* 61(2): 181–208

Dahl, Robert A. 1989. *Democracy and Its Critics*. New Haven, CT: Yale University Press.

2006. *On Political Equality*. New Haven, CT: Yale University Press.

Dahlberg, Stefan and Sören Holmberg. 2014. 'Democracy and Bureaucracy: How Their Quality Matters for Popular Satisfaction'. *West European Politics* 37: 515–17.

Dahlström, Carl, Peter Sundin and Jan Teorell. 2013. 'The Quality of Government Expert Survey 2008–2011: A Report'. QoG Working Paper 2013:15, The Quality of Government Institute, University of Gothenburg.

Dahlström, Carl, Victor Lapuente and Jan Teorell. 2011. 'The Merit of Meritocratization: Politics, Bureaucracy, and the Institutional Deterrents of Corruption'. *Political Research Quarterly* 65(3): 656–68.

De Beco, Gauthier. 2011. 'Monitoring Corruption from a Human Rights Perspective'. *International Journal of Human Rights* 15(7): 1107–24.

Della Porta, Donatella and Alberto Vannucci. 1999. *Corrupt Exchanges: Actors, Resources, and Mechanisms of Political Corruption*. New York: de Gruyter.

de Maria, William. 2010. 'Why Is the President of Malawi Angry? Towards an Ethnography of Corruption'. *Culture and Organization* 16(2): 145–62.

Diamond, Larry. 2007. 'A Quarter-Century of Promoting Democracy'. *Journal of Democracy* 18(4): 118–20.

Dryzek, John S., Bonnie Honig and Anne Phillips, eds. 2006. *The Oxford Handbook of Political Theory*. Oxford University Press.

du Gay, Paul. 2000. *In Praise of Bureaucracy: Weber, Organization and Ethics*. London: Sage.

Dworkin, Ronald. 1977. *Taking Rights Seriously*. London: Duckworth.

Edin, Maria. 2003. 'State Capacity and Local Agent Control in China. CCP Cadre Management from a Township Perspective'. *China Quarterly* 173: 35–52.

2005. 'Local State Structure and Developmental Incentives in China'. In *Asian States: Beyond the Developmental Perspective*, eds. R. Boyd and T. W. Ngo. London: RoutledgeCurzon.

Eisenstadt, S. N. and Roniger, Luis. 1984. *Patrons, Clients and Friends: Interpersonal Relations and the Structure of Trust in Society.* Cambridge University Press.

Erdmann, Gero and Ulf Engel. 2007. 'Neopatrimonialism Reconsidered: Critical Review and Elaboration of an Elusive Concept'. *Commonwealth & Comparative Politics* 45(1): 95–119.

Euben, J. Peter. 1989. 'Corruption'. In *Political Innovation and Conceptual Change*, eds. T. Ball, J. Farr and R. L Hanson. Cambridge University Press.

Evans, Peter and James E. Rauch. 1999. 'Bureaucracy and Growth: A Cross-National Analysis of the Effects of "Weberian" State Structures on Economic Growth'. *American Sociological Review* 64(5): 748–65.

and James E. Rauch. 2000. 'Bureaucratic Structure and Bureaucratic Performance in Less Developed Countries'. *Journal of Public Economics* 75: 49–71.

Evans, Richard J. 2009. *The Coming of the Third Reich*. Peterborough: Royal National Institute.

Fanon, Frantz. 1967. *The Wretched of the Earth*. Harmondsworth: Penguin Books.

Fehr, Ernst and Urs Fischbacher. 2005. 'The Economics of Strong Reciprocity'. In *Moral Sentiments and Material Interests: The Foundations for Cooperation in Economic Life*, eds. H. Gintis, S. Bowles, R. Boyd and E. Fehr. Cambridge, MA: MIT Press.

Friedrich, Carl J. 1972. *The Pathology of Politics, Violence, Betrayal, Corruption, Secrecy and Propaganda*. New York: Harper & Row.

Fukuyama, Francis. 2004. *State-Building: Governance and World Order in the Twenty-First Century*. Ithaca, NY: Cornell University Press.

2011. *The Origins of Political Order: From Prehuman Times to the French Revolution*. New York: Farrar, Straus & Giroux.

2012. 'Acemoglu and Robinson on Why Nations Fail (book review)'. *The American Interest*. 26 March 2012.

2013. 'What Is Governance?' *Governance: An International Journal of Policy, Administration and Institutions* 26(3): 347–68.

2014. *Political Order and Political Decay: From the Industrial Revolution to the Globalization of Democracy*. New York: Farrar, Straus & Giroux.

Gambetta, Diego. 2002. 'Corruption. An Analytical Map'. In *Political Corruption in Transition: A Skeptic's Handbook*, eds. S. Kolkin and A. Sajó. Budapest: Central European University Press.

Gao, Jie. 2009. 'Governing by Goals and Numbers: A Case Study in the Use of Performance Measurement to Build State Capacity in China'. *Public Administration and Development* 29(1): 21–31.

Gathii, James T. 2009. 'Defining the Relationship between Human Rights and Corruption'. *University of Pennsylvania Journal of International Law* 31: 125.

Gebeye, Berihun. 2012. 'Corruption and Human Rights: Exploring the Relationships'. Available at SSRN 2075766.

Génaux, Maryvonne. 2004. 'Social Sciences and the Evolving Concept of Corruption'. *Crime, Law and Social Change* 42(1): 13–24.

Gerring, John. 2012. *Social Science Methodology : A Unified Framework*, Vol. 2: *Strategies for Social Inquiry*. New York: Cambridge University Press.

and Joshua Ysenowitz. 2006. 'A Normative Turn in Political Science'. *Polity* 38: 101–33.

Gilley, Bruce. 2006. 'The Determinants of State Legitimacy: Results for 72 Countries'. *International Political Science Review* 27(1): 47–71.

2009. *The Right to Rule: How States Win and Lose Legitimacy*. New York: Columbia University Press.

Gjefsen, Torbjorn. 2012. 'Sources of Legitimacy: Quality of Government and Electoral Democracy'. Master thesis, Department of Political Science, University of Oslo.

Golden, Miriam. 2000. 'Political Patronage, Bureaucracy and Corruption in Postwar Italy'. Paper presented at the Annual Meeting of the American Political Science Association, Washington, August 28–September 2.

2003. 'Electoral Connections: The Effects of the Personal Vote on Political Patronage, Bureaucracy and Legislation in Post-War Italy'. *British Journal of Political Science* 33(2): 189–212.

Gong, Ting. 2011. 'An "Institutional Turn" in Integrity Management in China'. *International Review of Administrative Sciences* 77(4): 671–86.

Goodin, Robert E. 1982. *Political Theory and Public Policy*. Princeton, NJ: Princeton University Press.

2004. 'Democracy, Justice and Impartiality'. In *Justice and Democracy*, eds. K. Dowding, R. E. Goodin and C. Pateman. Cambridge University Press.

Greenberg, Stanley B. 2009. *Dispatches from the War Room: In the Trenches with Five Extraordinary Leaders*. New York: St Martin's Press.

Greif, Avner. 2005. 'Institutions and the Path to the Modern Economy: Lessons from Medieval Trade'. In *Handbook of Institutional Economics*, eds. C. Ménard and M. M. Shirley. Amsterdam: Springer.

Grzymala-Busse, Anna. 2008. 'Beyond Clientelism, Incumbent State Capture and State Formation'. *Comparative Political Studies* 41(4–5): 638–73.

Gustavson, Maria. 2014. *Auditing Good Government in Africa: Public Sector Reform, Professional Norms and the Development Discourse*. New York: Palgrave Macmillan.

Habyarimana, James P., Macartan Humphreys, Daniel N. Posner and Jeremy M. Weinstein. 2009. *Coethnicity: Diversity and the Dilemmas of Collective Action*. New York: Sage.

Hall, Peter A. and Michèle Lamont, eds. 2009. *Successful Societies: How Institutions and Culture Affect Health*. New York: Cambridge University Press.

Halleröd, Björn, Bo Rothstein, Adel Daoud and Shailen Nandy. 2013. 'Bad Governance and Poor Children: A Comparative Analysis of Government Efficiency and Severe Child Deprivation in 68 Low- and Middle-Income Countries'. *World Development* 48: 19–31.

He, Wei Ping. 2014. *Banking Regulation in China*. New York: Palgrave Macmillan.

Heberer, Thomas and Christian Göbel. 2011. *The Politics of Community Building in Urban China*. London: Routledge.

Heidenheimer, Arnold J. 2002. 'Perspectives on the Perception of Corruption'. In *Political Corruption: Concepts and Contexts*, eds. A. J. Heidenheimer and M. Johnston. New Brunswick, NJ: Transaction Publishers.

and Michael Johnston. 2002. *Political Corruption: Concepts and Contexts*, 3rd edn. New Brunswick, NJ: Transaction Publishers.

Michael Johnston and Victor T. Le Vine. 1989. *Political Corruption: A Handbook*. New Brunswick, NJ: Transaction Publishers.

Hellman, Joel S., Geraint Jones and Daniel Kaufmann. 2000. 'Seize the State, Seize the Day: State Capture, Corruption, and Influence in Transition'. Policy Research Paper 2444, World Bank Institute, Governance Regulation and Finance Division, Washington, DC.

Heywood, Paul M. 1997. 'Political Corruption: Problems and Perspectives'. *Political Studies* 45(3): 417–35.

2015. 'Introduction: Scale and Focus in the Study of Corruption'. In *Routledge Handbook of Political Corruption*, ed. P. M. Heywood. London: Routledge.

and Jonathan Rose. 2015. 'Curbing Corruption or Promoting Integrity? Probing the Hidden Conceptual Challenge'. In *Debates of Corruption and Intregrity*, eds. P. Hardi, P. M. Heywood and D. Torsello. New York: Palgrave Macmillan.

Hicken, Allen. 2011. 'Clientelism'. *Annual Review of Political Science* 14(1): 289–310.

Hilgers, Tina. 2011. 'Clientelism and Conceptual Stretching: Differentiating among Concepts and among Analytical Levels'. *Theory and Society* 40(5): 567–88.

Hill, Declan. 2008. *The Fix: Soccer and Organized Crime*. Toronto: McClelland & Stewart.

Hill, Michael J. and Peter L. Hupe. 2009. *Implementing Public Policy: Governance in Theory and Practice*. London: Sage.

Hindess, Barry. 2005. 'Investigating International Anti-Corruption'. *Third World Quarterly* 26(8): 1389–98.

Ho, Alfred Tai-Kei and Meili Niu. 2013. 'Rising with the Tide without Flipping the Boat: Analyzing the Successes and Challenges of Fiscal Capacity Building in China'. *Public Administration and Development* 33(1): 29–49.

Hodgkinson, Peter. 1997. 'The Sociology of Corruption: Some Themes and Issues'. *Sociology* 31(1): 17–35.

Holmberg, Sören and Bo Rothstein. 2011. 'Correlates of Democracy'. Working Paper 2011:10, Quality of Government Institute, University of Gothenburg.

     and Bo Rothstein, eds. 2012. *Good Government: The Relevance of Political Science*. Cheltenham: Edward Elgar.

     and Bo Rothstein. 2015. 'Good Societies Need Good Leaders on a Leash'. In *Elites, Institutions and the Quality of Government*, eds. C. Dahlstrom and L. Wängnerud. New York: Palgrave.

Hopkin, Jonathan. 2006. 'Conceptualizing Political Clientelism: Political Exchange and Democratic Theory'. Paper presented at the Annual Meeting of the American Political Science Association, Philadelphia, September 1–4.

Huang, Kai-Ping and Karen Y. Wang. 2011. 'How *Guanxi* Relates to Social Capital? A Psychological Perspective'. *Journal of Social Sciences* 7(2): 120–6.

Huntington, Samuel P. 1991. *The Third Wave: Democratization in the Late Twentieth Century*. Norman: University of Oklahoma Press.

Hydén, Göran. 2006. *African Politics in Comparative Perspective*. New York: Cambridge University Press.

Jackson, Robert H. and Carl G. Rosberg. 1982. 'Why Africa's Weak States Persist: The Empirical and Juridical in Statehood'. *World Politics* 35(1): 1–24.

Jain, Arvind K. 2001. 'Corruption: A Review'. *Journal of Economic Surveys* 15(1): 71–121.

Johnston, Michael. 1979. 'Patrons and Clients, Jobs and Machines: A Case Study of the Uses of Patronage'. *American Political Science Review* 73(2): 385–98.

1996. 'The Search for Definitions: The Vitality of Politics and the Issue of Corruption'. *International Social Science Journal* 48(149): 321–35.

2005. *Syndromes of Corruption: Wealth, Power, and Democracy.* Cambridge University Press.

2006. 'From Thucydides to Mayor Daley: Bad Politics, and a Culture of Corruption'. *Political Science and Politics* 39(4): 809–12.

2013. 'More than Necessary, Less than Sufficient: Democratization and the Control of Corruption'. *Social Research: An International Quarterly* 80(4): 1237–58.

Jordan, William Chester. 2009. 'Anti-Corruption Campaigns in Thirteenth-Century Europe'. *Journal of Medieval History* 35: 204–19.

Jordan Smith, Daniel. 2007. *A Culture of Corruption: Everyday Deception and Popular Discontent in Nigeria.* Princeton, NJ: Princeton University Press.

Joseph, Richard A. 1987. *Democracy and Prebendal Politics in Nigeria: The Rise and Fall of the Second Republic.* Cambridge University Press.

Karklins, Rasma. 2005. *The System Made Me Do It: Corruption in Post-Communist Societies.* Armonk, NY: M.E. Sharpe.

Katzarova, Elitza. 2011. 'The National Origin of the International Anti-Corruption Business'. Paper presented at International Studies Association Annual Convention, Montreal.

Kaufman, Herbert. 1960. *The Forest Ranger: A Study in Administrative Behavior.* Baltimore: Resources for the Future Press.

Kaufman, Robert R. 1972. 'The Patron-Client Concept and Macro-Politics: Prospects and Problems'. *Comparative Studies in Society and History* 16(3): 284–308.

Kaufmann, Daniel. 2008. *Daniel Kaufmann's Farewell Lecture: Governance, Crisis, and the Longer View: Unorthodox Reflections on the New Reality.* Washington, DC: World Bank.

and Pedro C. Vicente. 2011. 'Legal Corruption'. *Economics & Politics* 23(2): 195–219.

Art Kraay and Massimo Mastruzzi. 2004. 'Governance Matters III: Governance Indicators for 1996–2002'. World Bank Policy Research Working Paper 3106, Washington, DC.

Kawata, Jun'ichi. 2006. *Comparing Political Corruption and Clientelism.* Burlington, VT: Ashgate.

Keefer, P. 2007. 'Clientelism, Credibility, and the Policy Choices of Young Democracies'. *American Journal of Political Science* 51: 804–21.

Keping, Yu. 2014. 'Learning, Training and Governing: The CCP's Cadre Education since the Reform'. Paper presented at the International Conference Governance, Adaptability and System Stability under

One-Party Rule, China Center for Global Governance and Development, Nanchang University, March 27–29.

Kettering, Sharon. 1988. 'The Historical Development of Political Clientelism'. *Journal of Interdisciplinary History* 18(3): 419–47.

Khaldun, Ibn. 1958. *The Muqaddimah: An Introduction to History. Vol. I-III. Translated by Franz Rosenthal*. New York: Pantheon Books.

King, Desmond S. 1999. *In the Name of Liberalism: Illiberal Social Policy in the USA and Britain*. Oxford University Press.

Kitschelt, Herbert. 2000. 'Citizens, Politicians, and Party Cartellization: Political Representation and State Failure in Post-Industrial Democracies'. *European Journal of Political Research* 37: 149–79.

and Steven Wilkinson. 2007. 'Citizen-Politician Linkages: An Introduction'. In *Patrons, Clients, and Policies: Patterns of Democratic Accountability and Political Competition*, eds. Herbert Kitschelt and Steven Wilkinson. Cambridge University Press.

Kobayashi, Masaya. 2006. 'Political Corruption and Clientelism: Neo-Structuralism and Republicanism'. In *Comparing Political Corruption and Clientelism*, ed. J Kawata. Burlington, VT: Ashgate.

Koechlin, L. and M. Carmona. 2009. 'Corruption and Human Rights: Exploring the Connection'. In *Corruption, Global Security, and World Order*, ed. R. I. Rotberg. Washington, DC: Brookings Institution.

Kopecky, Petr and Gerardo Scherlis. 2008. 'Party Patronage in Contemporary Europe'. *European Review* 16(3): 355.

Peter Mair and Maria Spirova. 2012. *Party Patronage and Party Government in European Democracies*. Oxford University Press.

Kotkin, Stephen and András Sajó. 2002. *Political Corruption in Transition: A Sceptic's Handbook*. Budapest: Central European University Press.

Kurer, Oskar. 2005. 'Corruption: An Alternative Approach to Its Definition and Measurement'. *Political Studies* 53(1): 222–39.

Laegreid, Per and Tom Christensen. 2007. *Transcending New Public Management: The Transformation of Public Sector Reforms*. Burlington, VT: Ashgate.

Lambsdorff, Johann Graf. 2007. *The Institutional Economics of Corruption and Reform: Theory, Evidence, and Policy*. Cambridge University Press.

Landé, Carl H. 1983. 'Political Clientelism in Political Studies Retrospect and Prospects'. *International Political Science Review* 4(4): 435–54.

LaPalombara, Joseph. 1994. 'Structural and Institutional Aspects of Corruption'. *Social Research* 61(2): 325–50.

Lapuente, Victor and Bo Rothstein. 2014. 'Civil War Spain versus Swedish Harmony: The Quality of Government Factor'. *Comparative Political Studies* 47(10): 1416–41.

Ledberg, Sofia K. 2014. 'Governing the Military: Professional Autonomy in the Chinese People's Liberation Army'. PhD dissertation, Department of Government, Uppsala University.

Leff, Nathaniel H. 1964. 'Economic Development through Bureaucratic Corruption'. *American Behavioral Scientist* 8(3): 8–14.

Lessig, Lawrence. 2013. '"Institutional Corruption" Defined'. *Journal of Law, Medicine & Ethics* 41(3): 553–5.

Levi, Margaret, Audrey Sacks and Tom Tyler. 2009. 'Conceptualizing Legitimacy, Measuring Legitimating Beliefs'. *American Behavioral Scientist* 53(3): 354–75.

Levi-Faur, David. 2012. 'From "Big Government" to "Big Governance"'. In *Oxford Handbook of Governance*, ed. D. Levi-Faur. Oxford University Press.

Li, Ling. 2011. 'Performing Bribery in China: *Guanxi*-Practice, Corruption with a Human Face'. *Journal of Contemporary China* 20(68): 1–20.

Li, Shaomin M. and Judy J. Wu. 2010. 'Why Some Countries Thrive Despite Corruption: The Role of Trust in the Corruption-Efficiency Relationship'. *Review of International Political Economy* 17(1): 129–54.

Liou, Kuotsai Tom, Lan Xue and KeYong Dong. 2012. 'China's Administration and Civil Service Reform: An Introduction'. *Review of Public Personnel Administration* 32(2): 108–14.

Lovett, Frank. 2016. 'Republicanism'. In *The Stanford Encyclopedia of Philosophy* (Spring edn.), ed. Edward N. Zalta. Stanford Online.

Lynn, Laurence E., Jr. 2012. 'The Many Faces of Governance'. In *Oxford Handbook of Governance*, ed. D. Levi-Faur. Oxford University Press.

MacMullen, Ramsay. 1988. *Corruption and the Decline of Rome*. New Haven, CT: Yale University Press.

Mandela, Nelson. 1994. *Long Walk to Freedom: The Autobiography of Nelson Mandela*. London: Little Brown.

Mann, Michael. 2005. *The Dark Side of Democracy: Explaining Ethnic Cleansing*. New York: Cambridge University Press.

March, James B. and Johan P. Olsen. 1989. *Rediscovering Institutions: The Organizational Basis of Politics*. New York: Basic Books.

Marquette, Heather. 2014. 'Religion, Ethics and Corruption: Field Evidence from India and Nigeria'. In *Routledge Handbook of Political Corruption*, ed. P. M. Heywood. London: Routledge.

McCoy, Jennifer L. 2001. 'The Emergence of a Global Anti-Corruption Norm'. *International Politics* 38(1): 65–90.

Médard, J.-F., 1998. 'Postface'. In *Le clientélisme politique dans les sociétés contemporaines*, eds. J.-L. Briquet and F. Sawiki. Paris: Presses Universitaires de France.

Mueller, Dennis C. 1997. *Perspectives on Public Choice: A Handbook.* New York: Cambridge University Press.

Mill, John Stuart. 1861/1992. *On Liberty and Utilitarianism.* New York: Knopf.

Miller, Gary J. 1992. *Managerial Dilemmas: The Political Economy of Hierarchy.* Cambridge University Press.

Miller, Seumas. 2011. 'Corruption'. In *The Stanford Encyclopedia of Philosophy* (Spring edn.), ed. Edward N. Zalta. Stanford Online, available at http://plato.stanford.edu/archives/spr2011/entries/corruption/.

Miller, William L., B. Grødeland Åse and Tatyana Y. Koshechkina. 2001. *A Culture of Corruption? Coping with Government in Post-Communist Europe.* Budapest: Central European University Press.

Milner, Henry and Eskil Wadensjö, eds. 2001. *Gösta Rehn, the Swedish Model and Labour Market Policies: International and National Perspectives.* Aldershot: Ashgate.

Milovanovitch, Mihaylo. 2014. 'Fighting Corruption in Education'. In *World Bank Legal Review,* Vol. 5: *Fostering Development through Opportunity, Inclusion, and Equity,* eds. H. Cisse, N. R. M. Menon, M. C. C. Segger and V. O. Nmehielle. Washington, DC: World Bank.

Mintzberg, Henry. 2010. *The Structuring of Organizations.* Englewood Cliff, NJ: Prentice-Hall.

Møller, Jørgen and Svend-Erik Skaaning. 2014. *The Rule of Law: Definitions, Measures, Patterns and Causes.* Basingstoke: Palgrave Macmillan.

Mulgan, Richard. 2012. 'Aristotle on Legality and Corruption'. In *Corruption: Expanding the Focus,* eds. M. Barcham, B. Hindess and P. Larmour. Canberra: Australian National University Press.

Mungiu-Pippidi, Alina. 2006. 'Corruption: Diagnosis and Treatment'. *Journal of Democracy* 17(3): 86–99.

2015. *The Quest for Good Governance: How Societies Develop Control of Corruption.* New York: Cambridge University Press.

Muno, Wolfgang. 2010. 'Conceptualizing and Measuring Clientelism'. Paper presented at the Workshop Neopatrimonialism in Various World Regions, German Institute of Global and Area Studies (GIGA), Hamburg.

Myrdal, Gunnar. 1968. *Asian Drama: An Inquiry into the Poverty of Nations.* New York: Twentieth Century Fund.

Neier, Aryeh. 2002. *Taking Liberties: Four Decades in the Struggle for Rights.* New York: Public Affairs Press.

Nichols, Philip M., George J. Siedel and Matthew Kasdin. 2004. 'Corruption as a Pan-Cultural Phenomenon: An Empirical Study in Countries at

Opposite Ends of the Former Soviet Empire'. *Texas Journal of International Law* 39(2): 215–36.

Noonan, John Thomas. 1984. *Bribes*. New York: Macmillan.

Norris, Pippa. 2012. *Democratic Governance and Human Security: The Impact of Regimes on Prosperity, Welfare and Peace*. New York: Cambridge University Press.

2014. *Why Electoral Integrity Matters*. Cambridge University Press.

North, Douglass C. 1990. *Institutions, Institutional Change and Economic Performance*. Cambridge University Press.

1998. 'Economic Performance through Time'. In *The New Institutionalism in Sociology*, eds. M. C. Brinton and V. Nee. New York: Sage.

John J. Wallis and Barry R. Weingast. 2009. *Violence and Social Orders: A Conceptual Framework for Interpreting Recorded Human History*. Cambridge University Press.

Offe, Claus. 2009. 'Governance: An "Empty Signifier"?' *Constellations* 16(4): 550–61.

Olson, Mancur, Jr. 1965. *The Logic of Collective Action (Public Goods and the Theory of Groups)*. Cambridge, MA: Harvard University Press.

1996. 'Big Bills Left on the Sidewalk: Why Some Nations Are Rich, and Others Poor'. *Journal of Economic Perspectives* 10(2): 3–24.

Ostrom, Elinor. 1990. *Governing the Commons: The Evolution of Institutions for Collective Action*. New York: Cambridge University Press.

Ott, Jan C. 2010. 'Good Governance and Happiness in Nations: Technical Quality Precedes Democracy and Quality Beats Size'. *Journal of Happiness Studies* 11(3): 353–68.

Ottervik, Mattias. 2013. 'Conceptualizing and Measuring State Capacity'. QoG Working Paper 2013: 20, The Quality of Government Institute, University of Gothenburg.

Ouchi, William G. 1980. 'Markets, Bureaucracies and Clans'. *Administrative Science Quarterly* 25(1): 129–41.

Pearson, Zoe. 2013. 'An International Human Rights Approach to Corruption'. In *Corruption and Anti-Corruption*, eds. P. Larmour and N. Wolanin. Canberra: Asia Pacific Press.

Pellegrin, Pierre. 2012. 'Aristotle's *Politics*'. In *Oxford Handbook of Aristotle*, ed. C. Shields. Oxford University Press.

Persson, Anna, Bo Rothstein and Jan Teorell. 2013. 'Why Anti-Corruption Reforms Fail: Systemic Corruption as a Collective Action Problem'. *Governance: An International Journal of Policy, Administration and Institutions* 25(3): 449–71.

Philp, Mark. 1997. 'Defining Political Corruption'. *Political Studies* 45(3): 436–62.

2015. 'The Definition of Political Corruption'. In *Routledge Handbook of Political Corruption*, ed. P. M. Heywood. New York: Routledge.

Piattoni, Simona. 2001. 'Clientelism in Historical and Comparative Perspective'. In *Clientelism, Interests, and Democratic Representation*, ed. S. Piattoni (pp. 1–30). Cambridge University Press.

Pieke, Frank N. 2009. *The Good Communist: Elite Training and State Building in Today's China*. Cambridge University Press.

Pierre, Jon and B. Guy Peters. 2000. *Governance, Politics and the State*. New York: Macmillan.

and B. Guy Peters. 2005. *Governing Complex Societies: Trajectories and Scenarios*. Basingstoke: Palgrave Macmillan.

Pitcher, Anne, Mary H. Moran and Michael Johnston. 2009. 'Rethinking Patrimonialism and Neopatrimonialism in Africa'. *African Studies Review* 52(1): 125–56.

Pitkin, Hanna Fenichel. 1981. 'Justice: On Relating Private and Public'. *Political theory* 9(3): 327–52.

Popovski, Vesselin and G. Shabbir Cheema. 2010. *Engaging Civil Society: Emerging Trends in Democratic Governance*. Washington, DC: United Nations University Press.

Pritchett, Lant and Michael Woolcock. 2004. 'Solutions When the Solution Is the Problem: Arraying the Disarray in Development'. *World Development* 32(2): 191–212.

Pye, Lucian W. 1981. *The Dynamics of Chinese Politics*. Cambridge, MA: Oelgeschlager, Gunn & Hain.

Rajagopal, Balakrishnan. 1999. 'Corruption, Legitimacy and Human Rights: The Dialectic of the Relationship'. *Connecticut Journal of International Law* 14(2): 1–19.

Rawls, John. 1971. *A Theory of Justice*. Oxford University Press.

2005. *Political Liberalism* (expanded edn.). New York: Columbia University Press.

Ritner, Scott. 2011. 'The Concept of Corruption in Machiavelli's Political Thought'. Available at SSRN 1808959.

Rodrik, Dani. 1999. 'Institutions for High-Quality Growth: What They Are and How to Acquire Them'. Paper presented at International Monetary Fund Conference on Second Generation Reform, Washington, DC, November 8–9.

2007. *One Economics, Many Recipes: Globalization, Institutions and Economic Growth*. Princeton, NJ: Princeton University Press.

Arvind Subramanian, and Francesco Trebbi. 2004. 'Institutions Rule: The Primacy of Institutions over Geography and Integration in Economic Development'. *Journal of Economic Growth* 9(1): 131–65.

Roniger, Luis. 2004. 'Political Clientelism, Democracy, and Market Economy'. *Comparative Politics* 36(4): 353–75.

Rose-Ackerman, Susan. 1999. *Corruption and Government: Causes, Consequences, and Reform.* New York: Cambridge University Press.

and Tina Søreide, eds. 2011. *International Handbook on the Economics of Corruption*, Vol. 2. Cheltenham: Edward Elgar.

Rotberg, Robert I., ed. 2009. *Corruption, Global Security, and World Order.* Washington, DC: Brookings Institution.

2016. 'Corruption in America: From Benjamin Franklin's Snuff Box to Citizens United by Zephyr Teachout'. *Journal of Interdisciplinary History* 46(3): 453–5.

Roth, Guenther. 1968. 'Personal Rulership, Patrimonialism and Empire-Building in the New States'. *World Politics* 20(2): 194–206.

Rothstein, Bo. 1996. *The Social Democratic State: The Swedish Model and the Bureaucratic Problem of Social Reforms.* University of Pittsburgh Press.

1998. *Just Institutions Matter: The Moral and Political Logic of the Universal Welfare State.* Cambridge University Press.

2005. *Social Traps and the Problem of Trust.* Cambridge University Press.

2009. 'Creating Political Legitimacy: Electoral Democracy versus Quality of Government'. *American Behavioral Scientist* 53(3): 311–30.

2011. *The Quality of Government: Corruption, Social Trust and Inequality in a Comparative Perspective.* University of Chicago Press.

2012. 'Good Governance'. In *Oxford Handbook of Good Governance*, ed. D. Levi-Faur. Oxford University Press.

2014. 'What Is the Opposite of Corruption?' *Third World Quarterly* 35: 737–57.

2015. 'The Chinese Paradox of High Growth and Low Quality of Government: The Cadre Organization Meets Max Weber'. *Governance: An International Journal of Policy, Administration and Institutions* 28(4): 533–48.

and Dietlind Stolle. 2008. 'The State and Social Capital: An Institutional Theory of Generalized Trust'. *Comparative Politics* 40(3): 441–67.

and Marcus Tannenberg. 2015. 'Making Development Work: The Quality of Government Approach'. Report produced for the Swedish Government's Expert Group for Aid Analysis, Stockholm, Expertgruppen för biståndsanalys.

and Jan Teorell. 2008. 'What Is Quality of Government: A Theory of Impartial Political Institutions'. *Governance: An International Journal of Policy, Administration and Institutions* 21(2): 165–90.

and Jan Teorell. 2015. 'Causes of Corruption'. In *Routledge Handbook of Political Corruption*, ed. P. M. Heywood. London: Routledge.

and Davide Torsello. 2014. 'Bribery in Pre-Industrial Societies: Understanding the Universalism-Particularism Puzzle'. *Journal of Anthropological Research* 70(2): 263–82.

Sajó, Andras. 2003. 'From Corruption to Extortion: Conceptualization of Post-Communist Corruption'. *Crime, Law and Social Change* 40(2–3): 171–94.

Salmon Report. 1976. *Report of the Royal Commission on Standards of Conduct in Public Life*. Cmnd 6524. London: Her Majesty's Stationary Office.

Sandel, Michael J. 1999. 'Liberalism and Republicanism: Friends or Foes? A Reply to Richard Dagger'. *Review of Politics* 61(2): 209–14.

Sartori, Giovanni. 1970. 'Concept Misformation in Comparative Politics'. *American Political Science Review* 64(4): 1033–63.

Schedler, Andreas. 2002. 'The Menu of Manipulation'. *Journal of Democracy* 13(1): 36–50.

2010. *Concept Formation in Political Science*. Mexico City: CIDE.

Scott, James C. 1972. 'Patron-Client Politics and Political Change in Southeast Asia'. *American Political Science Review* 66(1): 91–113.

Sen, Amartya. 2009. *The Idea of Justice*. London: Allen Lane.

2011. 'Quality of Life: India vs. China'. *New York Review of Books* LVIII (25): 44–7.

Serra, Narcis and Joesph E. Stiglitz, eds. 2008. *The Washington Consensus Reconsidered: Towards a New Global Governance*. Oxford University Press.

Shah, Anwar. 2007. *Performance Accountability and Combating Corruption: Public Sector Governance and Accountability Series*. Washington, DC: World Bank.

Shirley, Mary M. 2005. 'Institutions and Development'. In *Handbook of Institutional Economics*, eds. C. Menard and M. M. Shirley. Amsterdam: Springer.

Shore, Cris and Dieter Haller. 2005. 'Sharp Practice: Anthropology and the Study of Corruption'. In *Corruption: Anthropological Perspectives*, eds. D. Haller and C. Shore. London: Pluto Press.

Shumer, Sara M. 1979. 'Machiavelli: Republican Politics and Its Corruption'. *Political Theory* 7(1): 5–34.

Singer, Matthew. 2009. 'Buying Voters with Dirty Money: The Relationship between Clientelism and Corruption'. Paper presented at the Annual Meeting of the American Political Science Association, Toronto, September 1–4.

Smith, B. C. 2007. *Good Governance and Development*. New York: Palgrave Macmillan.

Sneath, David. 2006. 'Transacting and Enacting Corruption, Obligation and the Use of Money in Mongolia'. *Ethnos* 71(1): 89–122.

Sorauf, Frank J. 1961. 'The Silent Revolution in Patronage'. In *Urban Government*, ed. E. Banfield. New York, Free Press.

Stine, Kelsi. 2011. 'A State of Inequality: Confronting Elite Capture in Post-Conflict Guatemala'. Master's thesis, Fletcher School of Law and Diplomacy, Tufts University, Boston.

Stokes, Suscan C. 2007. 'Political Clientelism'. In *Oxford Handbook of Comparative Politics*, eds. Carles Boix and Susan C. Stokes. Oxford University Press.

Strömberg, Håkan. 2000. *Allmän förvaltningsrätt*. Malmö: Liber.

Tebble, Adam James. 2002. 'What Is the Politics of Difference?' *Political Theory* 30(2): 259–81.

Teorell, Jan. 2010. *Determinants of Democratization: Explaining Regime Change in the World, 1972–2002*. Cambridge University Press.

2015. 'A Quality of Government Peace? Explaining the Onset of Militarized Interstate Disputes, 1985–2001'. *International Interactions* 41: 648–73.

Nicholas Charron, Stefan Dahlberg, Sören Holmberg, Bo Rothstein, Petrus Sundin and Richard Svensson. 2013. The Quality of Government Dataset, version 20 Dec. 2013, The Quality of Government Institute, University of Gothenburg, available at www.qog.pol.gu.se.

Theobald, Robin. 1982. 'Patrimonialism'. *World Politics* 34(4): 548–59.

Therborn, Göran. 2008. *What Does the Ruling Class Do When It Rules: State Apparatuses and State Power under Feudalism, Capitalism and Socialism*. London: Verso.

Thompson, Dennis F. 1995 *Ethics in Congress: From Individual to Institutional Corruption*. Washington, DC: Brookings Institution.

Torfing, Jacob B., Guy Peters, Jon Pierre and Eva Sorensen. 2012. *Interactive Governance: Advancing the Paradigm*. Oxford University Press.

Torsello, Davide. 2011. *The New Environmentalism? Civil Society and Corruption in the Enlarged EU*. London: Ashgate.

2015. 'Corruption as Social Exchange. The View from Anthropology'. In *Debates of Corruption and Integrity*, eds. Peter Hardi, Paul M. Heywood and Davide Torsello. New York: Palgrave Macmillan.

and Bertrand Vernand. 2016. 'The Anthropology of Corruption'. *Journal of Management Inquiry* 25(1): 34–54.

Tyler, Tom R. 1992. *Why People Obey the Law*. New Haven, CT: Yale University Press.

Underkuffler, Laura. 2005. 'Captured by Evil: The Idea of Corruption in Law'. Duke Law School Legal Studies Paper 83, Duke University, Durham, NC.

United Nations. 1998. *Annual Report of the Secretary-General on the Work of the Organization*, 27 August [online].

Uslaner, Eric M. and Bo Rothstein. 2016. 'The Historical Roots of Corruption: State Building, Economic Inequality, and Mass Education'. *Comparative Politics* 48(2): 216–27.

Van de Walle, Nicholas. 2000. *The Politics of Permanent Crisis: Managing African Economies*. New York: Cambridge University Press.

Van Klaveren, J. 1957. 'Corruption as a Historical Phenomenon'. In *Political Corruption: Concepts and Contexts*, eds. Arnold J. Heidenheimer and Michael Johnston. New Brunswick, NJ: Transaction Publishers.

Van Parijs, Philippe. 2011. *Just Democracy: Rhe Rawls-Machiavelli Programme*. Colchester: ECPR Press.

Varraich, Aiysha. 2014. 'Corruption: An Umbrella Concept'. Working Paper Series 2014:05, Quality of Government Institute, University of Gothenburg.

Versteeg, Mila and Tom Ginsburg. 2016. 'Measuring the Rule of Law: A Comparison of Indicators'. *Law & Social Inquiry* (online preview).

Von Alemann, Ulrich. 2004. 'The Unknown Depths of Political Theory: The Case for a Multidimensional Concept of Corruption'. *Crime, Law and Social Change* 42(1): 25–34.

Wang, Zhengxu. 2010. 'Citizens' Satisfaction with Government Performance in Six Asian-Pacific Giants'. *Japanese Journal of Political Science* 11: 51–75.

Weber, Max. 1922/1978. *Economy and Society: An Outline of Interpretive Sociology*. Berkeley: University of California Press.

Wedel, Janine R. 2014. *Unaccountable: How Anti-Corruption Watchdogs and Lobbyists Sabotaged America's Finance, Freedom and Security*. New York: Pegasus Books.

Wedeman, Andrew. 2012. *Double Paradox: Rapid Growth and Rising Corruption in China*. Ithaca, NY: Cornell University Press.

Weingrod, Alex. 1968. 'Patrons, Patronage, and Political Parties'. *Comparative Studies in Society and History* 10(4): 377–400.

Wenar, Leif. 2012. 'John Rawls'. In *Stanford Encyclopedia of Philosophy*, ed. E. N. Zalta. Stanford University Press.

Werner, Cynthia. 2000. 'Gifts, Bribes and Development in Post-Soviet Kazakstan'. *Human Organization* 59(1): 11–22.

Widmalm, Sten. 2005. 'Explaining Corruption at the Village Level and Individual Level in India'. *Asian Survey* XLV(5): 756–76.

2008. *Decentralisation, Corruption and Social Capital: From India to the West*. Thousand Oaks, CA: Sage.

Wildavsky, Aaron. 1973. 'If Planning Is Everything, Maybe It's Nothing'. *Policy Sciences* 4(2): 127–53.

Wolff, Jonathan. 2011. *Ethics and Public Policy: A Philosophical Inquiry*. New York: Routledge.

World Bank. 1997. *World Development Report 1997: The State in a Changing World*. New York: Oxford University Press.

2002. *World Development Report 2002: Building Institutions for Markets*. Washington, DC: World Bank.

2010. *Silent and Lethal: How Quiet Corruption Undermines Africa's Development Efforts*. Washington, DC: World Bank.

Wright, Bradley E., Donald P. Moynihan and Sanjay K. Pandey. 2012. 'Pulling the Levers: Transformational Leadership, Public Service Motivation, and Mission Valence'. *Public Administration Review* 72(2): 206–15.

You, Jong-Sung. 2007. 'Corruption as Injustice'. Paper presented at the Annual Meeting of the American Political Science Association, Chicago, August 31–September 3.

2015. *Democracy, Inequality and Corruption*. New York: Cambridge University Press.

Young, Iris M. 1990. *Justice and the Politics of Difference*. Princeton, NJ: Princeton University Press.

Zakaria, Fareed. 2003. *The Future of Freedom: Illiberal Democracy at Home and Abroad*. New York: W. W. Norton.

# Index

30452807R00103

Made in the USA
Lexington, KY
09 February 2019